PAUL D. SANSONE, O.F.M.

TITLES OF ADDRESS IN CHRISTIAN GREEK EPISTOLOGRAPHY TO 527 A. D.

TITLES OF ADDRESS IN CHRISTIAN GREEK EPISTOLOGRAPHY TO 527 A. D.

BY

SISTER LUCILLA DINNEEN

ARES PUBLISHERS INC.
CHICAGO   MCMLXXX

Exact Reprint of the Edition:
Washington, D.C. 1929
Ares Publishers Inc.
612 North Michigan Avenue
Chicago, Illinois 60611
Printed in the United States of America
International Standard Book Number
0-89005-376-6

PREFACE

One of the many subjects in the field of patristic Greek literature which have received little attention from scholars is that of titles of address. The only work which attempts to treat the subject as a whole from a study of the literary sources is the *Greek Lexicon of the Roman and Byzantine Periods* by E. A. Sophocles (First edition 1870; reprinted Cambridge 1914) but the information contained therein is obviously inadequate. Sister Agnes Clare Way in her work *The Language and Style of the Letters of St. Basil* (Washington 1927), has devoted a section to titles of address in St. Basil's letters. *The Vocabulary of the Greek Testament Illustrated from the Papyri and Other Non-Literary Sources* by Moulton and Milligan (London 1915—) records the New Testament words which occur as titles in papyri. The *Wörterbuch der griechischen Papyruskunden mit Einschluss der griechischen Inschriften, Ausschriften, Ostraka, Mumienschilder usw. aus Ägypten* by Preisigke (Berlin 1924—) when completed will contain a treatment of the titles which occur in non-literary sources. It is the aim of the present work to study titles of address as they are found in one of the literary sources for titles, the Christian epistolography of the first five centuries. These results are compared with the testimony of certain outstanding examples of pagan epistolography. Besides recording such lexicographical data as meaning, authors, frequency, and the recognition of words as titles, it aims especially to discover the social estate to which each title was attached. This phase of the study of titles of address has received practically no attention elsewhere.

Under the term, *titles of address*, I have included not only nouns and substantives which are titles in the exact sense, but also adjectives which have a conventional usage as titles of distinction or as epithets. The latter group may be considered as indirect titles.

The authors whose letters have been read in making this study are listed below.

*The Period from the Beginnings of Christian Literature to the
    Accession of Constantine (324 A. D.)*

The Epistles of the New Testament

*The Golden Age of Patristic Literature (Constantine 324 A. D.
    to the Council of Chalcedon 451 A. D.)*

    Epistola Encyclica
    Apologia contra Arianos (containing the letter of Arius to
        Alexander of Alexandria)
    Epistola de Nicaenis Decretis
    Epistola de Sententia Dionysi
    Epistola ad Dracontium
    Epistola ad Episcopos Aegypti et Libyae
    Apologia ad Imperatorem Constantium
    Apologia de Fuga Sua
    Epistola ad Serapionem de Morte Arii
    Epistola ad Monachos

---

[1] These letters contain no titles.

IV Epistolae ad Serapionem
Epistola de Synodis
Tomus ad Antiochenos
Epistola ad Jovianum
II Epistolae ad Orsisium
Epistola ad Afros
Epistola ad Epictetum
Epistola ad Adelphium
Epistola ad Maximum Philosophum
Epistola ad Joannem et Antiochum
Epistola ad Palladium
II Epistolae ad Amunem Monachum
Epistola Heortastica
Epistola ad Marcellum

    Among the letters of Cyril are found the letters of the fol-
lowing authors also studied: Acacius of Beroea; Alypius,
priest; Celestine of Rome; Maximianus of Constantinople;
Nestorius, the heresiarch; Paul of Emesa.

The Period of the Decline of Patristic Literature (from the Council of Chalcedon 451 A. D. to Justinian 527 A. D.)

Pseudo-Dionysius the Areopagite (10 letters) . . written probably
                                                    between 485-515
Gennadius of Constantinople (synodal letter) . . . . .d. c. 471

Pagan Authors

Julian the Apostate (87 letters) 331-363
Libanius of Antioch (1065 letters) . . . . .314- c. 393

By the *authors of importance* to whom I have referred in several places, I mean the Christian authors whose epistolary remains are extensive; they are Athanasius, Basil, Gregory of Nazianzus, Gregory of Nyssa, John Chrysostom, Synesius, Isidorus, Nilus, Cyril of Alexandria, and Theodoret. A few isolated letters which did not contribute appreciable materials have been omitted. The two pagan authors of letters included here have also been consulted because of their close literary and social contact with Christian writers, and the likelihood therefore of their using titles of address current among Christians.

I have used the text found in the Migne Patrologia, with the following exceptions:

St. Basil, The Letters, Volumes I and II, R. J. Deferrari, London, 1926-1928. I have used the Deferrari text for the letters so far as published, but for the sake of consistency, I have given all references to the letters of St. Basil from the Benedictine edition.

S. Patris Nostri Basilii, Opera Omnia, Tome III, Benedictine edition, Paris, 1721-1730. A second edition by Garnier and Maran, Paris, 1839. I did not use the Migne reprint.

Gregorii Nysseni Opera, Volume VIII, Fascicle II, G. Pasquali, Berlin, 1925.

Libanius, Volumes X and XI, R. Foerster, Leipsig, 1921-1922.

Eusebius Werke, Volumes II and IV, T. Mommsen, Leipsig, 1902-1908. These volumes contain the letters of Phileas of Thmuis, Irenaeus, Alexander of Jerusalem, and the letter of Eusebius to Flacillus.

Theodoret Kirchengeschichte, L. Parmentier, Leipsig, 1911. The
letters of Arius to Eusebius of Nicomedea, of Eusebius of
Caesarea to the Caesareans, and of Peter of Alexandria are
found here in Theodoret.

The Works of the Emperor Julian, Volume III, W. C. Wright,
London, 1923.

The Apostolic Fathers, Volumes I and II, Kirsopp Lake, New
York-London, 1911-1917. I have used this text for the let-
ters of Clement of Rome, Pseudo-Barnabas, Ignatius, and
Polycarp, and for the Epistle to Diognetus.

References from the Patrologia and St. Basil are made to letters by Roman numerals, to columns and sections in the usual
manner. For St. Athanasius, the number of the volume in the
Migne series is given in italics, followed by the column and section as above, for example, *25* 347 C. For Isidorus and Nilus, the
Roman numeral indicates the number of the book; the first arabic,
the number of the letter; the column and section are given as for
the other authors. For the letters of Libanius, I have followed
Foerster's notation—Greek numerals for the letter, and arabics
for the section. Other references will be readily understood.

The word ἀδελφός, which occurs so frequently in Christian Greek,
has been purposely omitted.

Besides the works mentioned above, the following have also been
found helpful:

Bardenhewer, Otto. *Geschichte der Altkirchlichen Litteratur,* IV
Volumes. Freiburg im Breisgau, 1912-1924.

Christ, W. von. *Geschichte der Griechischen Litteratur* umgear-
beitet von W. Schmid und O. Stählin, Zweiter Teil, Zweiter
Hälfte, von 100 bis 530 nach Christus. Sexte Auflage,
München, 1924.

Liddell, H. G., and Scott, R. *A Greek-English Lexicon.* Eighth
edition, New York, 1897. *A New Edition,* revised and aug-
mented by H. S. Jones, with the assistance of R. Mackenzie.
Parts I, II, III (α to ἐξευτελιστής). Oxford, 1925-1927.

Cremer, H. *Biblico-Theological Lexicon of New Testament
Greek.* Fourth English edition translated from the German
by W. Urwick. New York, 1895.

Thayer, J. W. *A Greek-English Lexicon of the New Testament.*
New York. No date.
Smith and Wace. *A Dictionary of Christian Biography.* Lon-
don, 1877.

The general conclusions adduced from the evidence presented in
this study I believe to be sound, as I have endeavored not to gen-
eralize where the evidence seemed too scanty to justify it. Com-
plete gaps and incomplete statements will, of course, be filled out
as new evidence appears.

The subject was suggested to me by Dr. Roy Joseph Deferrari,
Head of the Department of Greek and Latin of the Catholic University of America, to whom it was suggested in turn by Professor
Edward Capps of Princeton University out of his experience as
editor of the Loeb Classical Library. My sincere appreciation and
gratitude are extended to Dr. Deferrari for the suggestion and for
the careful direction he has given my investigations. I would
acknowledge also with many thanks, the assistance rendered by
the Reverend James Marshall Campbell, Associate Professor of
Latin and Greek, and the Reverend Arthur Adolphe Vaschalde,
Professor of Semitic Languages and Literatures, through their
reading of the manuscript.

To my superior, Mother Mary Domitilla, and to the Sisters of
my Congregation, I would express my deep indebtedness, for it is
to their interest in scholarship, to their kindness and encourage-
ment, that I owe the realization of my work.

SISTER LUCILLA.

Feast of Saint Joseph,
March 19, 1929.

TABLE OF CONTENTS

INTRODUCTION

TITLES OF ADDRESS

The essence of the title of address, which is so typical of Byzantine style, is, in the case of titles which are nouns, the identifying of a person with a complimentary quality, or, in the case of titles which are adjectives or substantives, the attributing of the quality to him. It is clear that the characteristic qualities and virtues of the various stations in life differ. Ἐξουσία is indeed appropriate to a governor, but θεοσέβεια would be considered more fitting for a bishop, while a woman would be more complimented by the possession of κοσμιότης. It is reasonable, therefore, to look for distinctive titles for the various classes and ranks in society, even as is the case with titles in modern usage. As the titles became more conventional, they lost the full significance of the quality which was expressed in them and became, in general, merely indicative of the class of persons to whom they were ordinarily addressed. For example, the title ὁσιότης expressed to the Byzantine mind, not " you are a holy man ", but rather " you are a bishop ".

Needless to say, the qualities expressed in a Byzantine title are far more varied and extravagant than those to which we are accustomed. Accordingly, we often have in English no title equivalent to that of the Greek, but we must be satisfied with expressions which sound strange to modern ears—expressions, nevertheless, which we cannot ignore if our aim is to recover Byzantium as far as may be.

CHAPTER I

Ecclesiastical Titles

Titles generally restricted in their use to members of the clergy are designated as ecclesiastical titles. They are divided into two classes, titles reserved for bishops, and titles applied to the clergy in general.

Titles of Bishops [1]

The hierarchy were honored with many complimentary titles. Those which were regularly addressed to bishops, with rare exceptions, are listed below.

ἁγιότης: n., *Sanctity.*

The title ἁγιότης is regularly addressed to bishops. Theodoret alone makes frequent use of it. There are a few examples in the less important contemporary authors, a fact which seems to indicate that the use of ἁγιότης as a title began about the latter part of the fifth century. Milligan cites it in a late sixth century papyrus, addressed by one bishop to another. Sophocles gives a citation of this usage from Theognostus Monachus, ninth century. The numerous examples of its being addressed to the patriarch of Alexandria by Theodoret and other inferior bishops, and the fact that Theodoret uses it for the bishops of Rome, Constantinople, Antioch, and sees that were more important than Cyrus, would lead us to believe that ἁγιότης was employed in addressing ecclesiastical superiors.

The title is used most commonly for the patriarch of Alexandria, for example: γέγραφα πρὸς τὴν σὴν ἁγιότητα, Synesius LXVII 1432 B; ἀποσταλέντα παρὰ τῆς σῆς ἁγιότητος γράμματα, Celestine of Rome 89 B; παρακαλῶν σου τὴν ἁγιότητα, Theodoret LX 1232 C; cf. also Synesius LXVII 1421 C; John of Antioch II 132 B; Celestine of Rome 89 C, 93 B; Paul of Emesa, 165 D; Firmus XXXVII 1508 A; Theodoret LXXXIII 1268 B.

---

[1] For titles used rarely or not exclusively in addressing bishops, cf. Index under *bishops.*

1

The remaining examples of the title are as follows: to Pope Leo, καὶ ἱκετεύω καὶ ἀντιβολῶ τὴν σὴν ἁγιότητα, Theodoret CXIII 1316 D, 1317 D; to the bishop of Constantinople, καὶ ἤδη σου τὴν ἁγιότητα δι' ἑτέρων ἐδίδαξα γραμμάτων, Theodoret CIV 1297 A and also XI 1184 C, XLVII 1224 C, LXXXVI 1281 A; to the bishops of Antioch, πλὴν ὀλίγων τῶν ὑπηρετουμένων τῇ σῇ ἁγιότητι κληρικῶν, letter of the emperors to John of Antioch 1461 A, and also Theodoret CX 1305 D, CXII 1312 B; to Andreas of Samosata in Theodoret XXIV 1205 A; to Eusebius of Ancyra in Theodoret LXXXII 1265 B; to bishops whose sees are uncertain in Theodoret CXVII [2] 1325 C, CLXX 1477 A and 1481 A.

Theodoret addresses the title once to the archimandrite Marcellus: καὶ νῦν δὲ πάλιν προσφθεγγόμεθά σου τὴν ἁγιότητα, CXLII 1365 D.

Serapion of Thmuis has a doubtful use of ἁγιότης as a title addressed to monks: οὐδ' αὖ πάλιν ἕτεραι πόλεις διεστράφησαν εὐμοιροῦσαι τῆς ὑμῶν ἁγιότητος, 929 B.

ἁγιωσύνη: n., *Sanctity*.

This title is common only in Theodoret. Like ἁγιότης, it is used for bishops, and the examples point to its being addressed ordinarily to ecclesiastical superiors. Its use as a title seems to have begun about Theodoret's time. It is also cited as occurring in papyri.[3]

In the following passages, ἁγιωσύνη is addressed to Leo of Rome: ἱκετεύομέν σου τὴν ἁγιωσύνην, Theodoret CXIII 1316 A, also 1313 C, 1316 A, 1317 C. It is applied also to Renatus, who was the Pope's representative at the Council of Ephesus: διά τοι τοῦτο τὴν ὑμετέραν ἁγιωσύνην παρακαλῶ, Theodoret CXVI 1324 D and also CXVIII 1328 A. There are several examples addressed to the bishops of Alexandria: ὃς καὶ τὰ γράμματα τῆς ἐμῆς βραχύτητος ἐπιδίδωσι τῇ σῇ ἁγιωσύνῃ, Alypius 148 C; τῆς γὰρ χρείας ὁ περὶ τὴν σὴν ἁγιωσύνην πόθος πλέον μοι ἔγκειται συντόνως τὴν ὁδὸν ἐξανῦσαι, John of Antioch II 132 B; cf. also Acacius 101 B and C; Alypius 148 A;

---

[2] There are several opinions concerning the addressee of this letter; all agree, however, that it was written to a bishop or to bishops.

[3] Liddell and Scott, new edition s. v.; Milligan and Moulton s. v.; Preisigke s. v.

Theodoret LX 1232 B, LXXXIII 1273 D.   The remaining examples are as follows: to the bishops of Constantinople, Theodoret XI 1184 B, XLVII 1225 B, LXXXVI 1280 C, CIV 1300 B; to the bishop of Antioch in Theodoret XXXI 1209 B; to the bishop of Ancyra, Theodoret LXXXII 1264 A and 1265 C, CIX 1301 D and 1304 B; to the bishop of Tyre in Theodoret XXXV 1213 A; to bishops of unknown sees, Theodoret CXII 1312 D, CXVII 1325 C, CLXX 1476 B, CLXX 1477 C.

Theodoret uses ἁγιωσύνη as a title once in a letter addressed to some eastern monks: διὸ τὴν ὑμετέραν ἁγιωσύνην παρακαλῶ, CLI 1432 B.

ἁγιώτατος: adj., *most saintly;* as a substantive, *most saintly Sir.*

Ἁγιώτατος as a title of distinction is generally applied to bishops. It occurs for the most part 'n writers of the fifth century, frequently in Theodoret and occasionally in Cyril of Alexandria. Basil makes use of it once in referring to a synod, CXLI 234 B.

The letters afford us numerous illustrations of the use of ἁγιώτατος as a title for bishops, nearly all addressed to ecclesiastical superiors as in the case of the corresponding noun title of address, ἁγιότης. For the bishops of Rome, there are the following examples: τοῦ ἁγιωτάτου καὶ ὁσιωτάτου τῆς Ῥωμαίων ἐπισκόπου τοῦ κυρίου Λέοντος, Theodoret CXLIV 1373 C; cf. also John of Antioch I 1452 B; Cyril of Alexandria XVII 108 C; Theodoret CXVI 1324 D and 1325 B, CXVIII 1328 B, CXXI 1532 A, CXLV 1384 D.   For the bishops of Constantinople, the title occurs as follows: τοῦ ἁγιωτάτου καὶ θεοφιλεστάτου τῆς Κωνσταντινουπολιτῶν ἐπισκόπου τοῦ κυρίου Φλαβιανοῦ, Theodoret CXIII 1316 A; cf. also Constantius among the letters of Chrysostom CCXXXVII 743, Paul of Emesa 168 A, Cyril of Alexandria XLIX 253 B.   It is addressed frequently to the bishops of Alexandria: τὸν ἁγιώτατον ἐπίσκοπον τῆς Ἀλεξανδρείας Κύριλλον, letter of the emperors to John of Antioch VI 1460 C; cf. also Synesius IX 1345 C; Nestorius 44 A; John of Antioch II 132 B, IV 169 D, V 248 A, VI 1460 C and 1461 A; Acacius 100 B; Alypius 145 C, 145 D, 148 B; Maximianus 149 C; Paul of Emesa 165 B.   The title is given to the bishops of Antioch in the following instances: Ἰωάννου ἁγιωτάτου ἐπισκόπου, Cyril of Alexandria XXIII 136 C; cf. also Acacius 101 C; Paul of Emesa 165 B; Theodoret XLIII 1220 D, LXXXI 1261 A, LXXXIII 1268 B. Ἁγιώτατος also occurs with the following uses: to Acacius of Beroea, the most aged and respected bishop of his time, τῷ ἁγιωτάτῳ καὶ θεοφιλεστάτῳ ἐπισκόπῳ πατρὶ ἡμῶν Ἀκακίῳ, John of Antioch IV 172 A and also Paul of Emesa 165 C; for several bishops or bishops in general, Cyril of Alexandria LXXXV 376 C, 377 A, and also Theodoret CXIX 1329 B, CLII 1441 B, CLIV 1445 B, CLVI 1449 B, CLVII 1452 C. For bishops of inferior or unknown sees, there are the following examples: Nilus II 60, 225 D; Cyril of Alexandria XXIII 136 A; John of Antioch IV 172 A, VI 1460 B; Theodoret CXI 1308 B, CXVII 1325 D, CLXX 1476 B, 1480 D, 1481 B.

The few instances when ἁγιώτατος is not applied to bishops are as follows: to archimandrites, οἱ θεοσεβέστατοι καὶ ἁγιώτατοι ἀρχιμανδρῖται, Cyril of Alexandria XXVIII 144 B; to a noted ascetic, ὁ ὁσιώτατος καὶ ἁγιώτατος ἄνθρωπος τοῦ Θεοῦ, ὁ κύριος Ἰάκωβος, Theodoret XLII 1220 B and XLIV 1221 D; to monks, τῶν παρ᾽ ἡμῖν ἁγιωτάτων μοναζόντων, Theodoret LXXXI 1264 A.

There is one uncertain case: Theodoret CXXX 1348 B. The person to whom the title is addressed is unknown but, from the context, he is probably a bishop.

ἀκρίβεια: n., *Precision.*

The title occurs rarely. It is addressed to bishops in the following instances: ἐκεῖνο δέ μοι καὶ φοβερὸν καὶ πολλῆς φροντίδος ἄξιον ἔδοξε, τὸ τὴν σὴν ἀκρίβειαν, ἣν ἐν ὀλίγοις ἐρείσμά τε ὀρθότητος ... σώζεσθαι πεπιστεύκαμεν, ἐπὶ τοσοῦτον τῆς παρούσης καταστάσεως μετασχεῖν, Basil XXV 104 A; ἱκανῶς δέ μου κἀκεῖνο τὴν ψυχὴν παρεκάλεσε, τὸ προστεθὲν παρὰ τῆς σῆς ἀκριβείας τοῖς λοιποῖς καλῶς καὶ ἀκριβῶς θεολογηθεῖσι, Basil CCLVIII 394 D; οὓς ἀξιοῦμεν παρὰ τῆς ὑμετέρας ἀκριβείας πρὸς πάσας τὰς κατὰ τὴν ἀνατολὴν ἐκκλησίας δημοσιευθῆναι, Basil CCLXIII 405 C; τὰ δὲ λοιπὰ εἰ μέν τινα σοφίαν κεκρυμμένης ἐπήγετο ταῖς τῶν ἀναγινωσκόντων ἀκοαῖς ἀκατάληπτον, τῆς σῆς ἐστιν ἀκριβείας εἰδέναι, Nestorius 52 D.

Basil addresses the title to the church of Neocaesarea: ὥστε ὁ τὴν πρὸς ἡμᾶς κοινωνίαν ἀποδιδράσκων, μὴ λανθανέτω ὑμῶν τὴν ἀκρίβειαν, πάσης ἑαυτὸν τῆς Ἐκκλησίας ἀπορρηγνύς, CCIV 307 C.

ἄνθρωπος τοῦ Θεοῦ: n., *man of God*.

The Biblical phrase ὁ ἄνθρωπος τοῦ Θεοῦ, is used by Byzantine writers as a title of special esteem. It occurs in the following passages of the Epistles of the New Testament: in reference to prophets, ὑπὸ Πνεύματος Ἁγίου φερόμενοι ἐλάλησαν οἱ ἅγιοι Θεοῦ ἄνθρωποι, II Peter I 21; and as a title of direct address to Timothy, σὺ δέ, ὦ ἄνθρωπε Θεοῦ, ταῦτα φεῦγε, I Timothy VI 11. In Byzantine times the expression was used generally in addressing bishops: κυρίῳ ποθεινοτάτῳ, ἀνθρώπῳ Θεοῦ, πιστῷ ὀρθοδόξῳ Εὐσεβίῳ, Ἄρειος ὁ διωκόμενος ὑπὸ Ἀλεξάνδρου, Arius quoted in Theodoret H. E. I 5, 1; ἄγε τοίνυν, ὦ Θεοῦ ἄνθρωπε, Basil CXCVII 288 A; οὐκ ἐν καλοῖς, ὦ ἄνθρωπε τοῦ Θεοῦ, τὰ ἡμέτερα, Gregory of Nyssa I 1; cf. also Basil CCXIV 321 B, Gregory of Nyssa XXV 17, Theodoret CXII 1309 B. There is one instance where the name of the addressee is lost, but he was probably a bishop: Theodoret CXXX 1348 B.

Theodoret addresses it to a famous ascetic: τὸν γνήσιον αὐτοῦ δοῦλον, τὸν ἁγιώτατον ἄνθρωπον τοῦ Θεοῦ τὸν κύριον Ἰάκωβον, XLIV 1221 D; cf. also XLII 1220 B.

A parallel expression, ἄνθρωπος τοῦ Κυρίου, occurs once in Nilus, addressed to a priest: καὶ ἡμεῖς πάνυ τὸ αὐτὸ ἐπευχόμεθά σοι, ἄνθρωπε τοῦ Κυρίου, III 7, 368 D.

γνησιότης: n., *Sincerity*.

As a title γνησιότης is very rare. John of Antioch uses it twice in addressing patriarchs: to Nestorius of Constantinople, καὶ ἐπειδή, ὡς νομίζω, πάσης εἰμὶ ὑποψίας λοιπὸν παρ᾽ ὑμῖν ἐκτός, ἀληθέσιν ἀπολογίαις χρησάμενος, πεπαρρησιασμένῃ λοιπὸν χρῶμαι πρὸς τὴν σὴν γνησιότητα συμβουλίᾳ, I 1450 A; πάντας τοὺς κυρίους θεοφιλεστάτους ἐπισκόπους τῆς Ἀνατολῆς συνάψαι τῇ φίλῃ ἐμοὶ καὶ τιμίᾳ κεφαλῇ τῆς σῆς φημι γνησιότητος, V 248 B.

Basil addresses it to a certain Theodorus who is unidentified but, from the context of the letter, we may suppose him to be a clergyman: καὶ ἐν δίχα τούτων συνέβη τῇ σῇ με περιτυχεῖν γνησιότητι, ἐλογισάμην ἂν ἐν σοὶ κἀκείνους ἑωρακέναι, CXXIV 214 C.

Γνησιότης is cited as a title in papyri.[4]

---

[4] Liddell and Scott, new edition s. v.; Preisigke s. v.

ἐπίσημος: adj., *notable.*

The examples of ἐπίσημος as a title are rare and are found only in authors of the fifth century. In the following passages, it is addressed to metropolitan bishops: ὡς καὶ τῶν ἐπισήμων μητροπολιτῶν καὶ θεοσεβεστάτων ἐπισκόπων, Cyril of Alexandria XXIII 135 B and also 136 B. John of Antioch addresses it to bishops: πολλοῖς καὶ πόνοις ἀγίων καὶ ἐπισήμων ἐπισκόπων, I 1453 A.

εὐσπλαγχνία: n., *Compassion.*

No examples of the use of εὐσπλαγχνία have been noted except in the letters of St. Basil. It is addressed to bishops as follows: τούτων μίαν προσεδοκήσαμεν λύσιν τὴν τῆς ὑμετέρας εὐσπλαγχνίας ἐπίσκεψιν, LXX 164 A; ὃν ὑπὸ τῆς σῆς εὐσπλαγχνίας παρακαλοῦμεν κατασχεθῆναι ἀπὸ τῆς βλαβερᾶς ταύτης ὁρμῆς, CXIX 211 C; ἔπρεπε δήπου καὶ ἡμῖν ἐν πολλῷ χρόνῳ πεπονηκόσι συνδιατεθῆναι τὴν εὐσπλαγχνίαν ὑμῶν, CCXLII 371 D. In the following instance, the addressee is unidentified: ταύτης αὐτοῖς τῆς πληροφορίας παρὰ τῆς εὐσπλαγχνίας ὑμῶν προτεθείσης, καὶ αὐτοὶ τὴν πρέπουσαν ὑμῖν ὑποταγὴν ἑτοιμοί εἰσι παρασχέσθαι, CXIV 207 C.

θεοσέβεια: n., *Godliness.*

Θεοσέβεια is found very frequently as a title of address. It occurs in almost all of the authors of the fourth and fifth centuries. Of the more important writers, Nilus alone does not make use of it. It is generally addressed to bishops, but there are a few illustrations of its use for other members of the clergy and for the emperor. Θεοσέβεια is cited as a title in papyri.[5]

Examples of the use of θεοσέβεια in addressing bishops are as follows: ἅμα γὰρ ὁ παρὰ τῆς ὑμετέρας θεοσεβείας καὶ τῶν ἀπανταχοῦ ὀρθοδόξων ἐπισκόπων πολλάκις ἀπαγορευθεὶς Λούκιος τῆς πρὸς αὐτὸν ἀπεχθῶς διακειμένης ἐπ᾽ εὐλόγοις ταῖς προφάσεσιν ἐπέστη πόλεως, Peter II of Alexandria quoted in Theodoret H. E. IV 22, 11; ὁ μέντοι συνδιάκονος ἡμῶν διηγήσεταί σου τῇ θεοσεβείᾳ, Basil C 196 A; γνώμῃ δε πολλάκις ἐπεστάλκαμέν σου τῇ θεοσεβείᾳ, Chrysostom CXLII 636; γινωσκέτω δὲ καὶ τοῦτο ἡ σὴ θεοσέβεια, Cyril of Alexandria XI 84 A. Cf. also Alexander of Alexandria II 577 B; Athanasius 25 324 A, 353 B,

---

[5] Moulton and Milligan s. v.; Preisigke s. v.

561 B, 685 A, and *26* 1052 C, 1053 C, 1072 A, 1073 A, 1181 A;
Basil XXVII 106 A, XXX 110 A, XLVIII 141 C, L 142 D, LVII
151 A, LIX 154 D, LXI 156 A, LXVI 159 D, LXIX 162 B,
LXXIX 173 A, LXXXIX 181 A, XCII 186 B, XCV 189 A and
B, XCVIII 192 B, C 196 B, CXX 211 D, CXXIX 221 B,
CXXXVIII 229 B and D, CXLI 234 D, CLXII 253 B, CLXV
255 E, CLXVI 256 D, CXC 283 A and B, CXCVIII 289 C, 290 A,
CCXVII 325 E, CCXVIII 331 A, CCXVIII 331 E, CCXXXI
354 A, CCXXXII 355 A, CCXXXVII 365 A and C, CCLIV
389 D, CCLXVII 413 D, 414 A, CCLXVIII 414 C; Gregory of
Nazianzus LXIV 125 C, LXV [6] 128 B, LXVI [6] 129 C, CLXXXII
279 A, CLXXXVI 305 C; Gregory of Nyssa I 5; Chrysostom
XXV 626, CXIV 671, CCXXX 737, CCXXXII 738; Synesius
LXVII 1412 C, 1424 C, 1432 A, LXXXIX 1456 D; Isidorus II
21, 472 A; Cyril of Alexandria II 40 C, 41 A, 41 B, 41 C, 41 D,
IV 44 C, XI 80 B, 80 C, 81 A, 84 D, XIII 93 C, 96 C, 96 D, XVI
105 A, XXXI 153 C, XLI 201 C, 201 D, 204 C, 220 D, XLV 237 A,
237 B, XLVIII 249 B, LXIII 328 C, LXXVI 353 B, 353 C,
353 D, 356 A, 357 A, 357 B, 357 C, LXXVII 360 A, LXXIX
365 B, LXXXII 376 A, LXXXIII 1075 A, 1077 A, LXXXIV
385 B, 388 A; Nestorius 44 A, 49 C; Acacius 100 B, 101 C; Paul
of Emesa 168 B; Atticus 349 C; John of Antioch I 1450 A, 1453 C,
IV 172 B, V 248 A, 248 B, VI 1460; Proclus XIII 884 B, 884 C;
Firmus XIV 1492 B, 1492 C, XV 1493 A, XIX 1496 A, XXII
1497 C, XXIII 1497 C, XXXIV 1505 A, XXXV 1505 B, XLI
1509 B, XLII 1509 B, 1509 C; Theodoret XVI 1193 B, XXXII
1209 D, XXXV 1212 D, XLVIII 1225 B, LXX 1240 C, LXXVII
1249 A, LXXVIII 1252 C, LXXXV 1276 D, 1277 B, CII 1296 B,
CXXX 1341 D, CXXXIII 1349 D, 1352 B, CXXXV 1356 A,
CXLVI 1412 C, CLXX 1476 B, 1480 C.

The following are examples of the title in the third person,
referring to bishops: καὶ χάριν ὡμολογήσαμεν τῇ θεοσεβείᾳ αὐτοῦ τε
καὶ τῶν συνελθόντων ἐν τῇ μεγάλῃ Ῥώμῃ, Athanasius *26* 1045 D; ταύτῃ
τοι γέγραφα πρὸς τὴν θεοσέβειαν αὐτοῦ, Cyril of Alexandria XL 200 B;
cf. also Athanasius *26* 797 B, Cyril of Alexandria VIII 60 B,
XLIX 256 A, and Theodoret LXXXVI 1277 C, 1280 A.

---

[6] Letters LXV and LXVI of St. Gregory appear also in the Basilian
corpus as letters CLXVI and CLXVII.

Theodoret addresses θεοσέβεια twice to an oeconomus: χρησάσθω τοίνυν ἡ σὴ θεοσέβεια, CV 1300 C and also CVI 1300 D.

There are several instances of its use as a title for archimandrites: παραιτεῖται ἡ σὴ θεοσέβεια μέχρι σήμερον τὴν πρὸς τὸν εὐσεβέστατον Ἰωάννην κοινωνίαν, Cyril of Alexandria LVII 320 C; τὴν ὑμετέραν θεοσέβειαν τοῦτο σὺν ἡμῖν παρακαλοῦμεν ποιεῖν, Theodoret CXXXVII 1357 D; cf. also Cyril of Alexandria LVI 320 A, 320 B, LVIII 321 B, 321 D; Theodoret CXXVII 1340 C, CXXXI 1348 D, CXLI 1365 A, 1365 C, 1365 D, CXLII 1568 C.

It is addressed to priests in the following passages: διὸ καὶ πολλὰς ἔχω χάριτας τῇ θεοσεβείᾳ τῇ σῇ, Chrysostom XCI 656; ὁ τῇ σῇ θεοσεβείᾳ προσφέρων τουτὶ τὸ γράμμα, Isidorus V 457, 1592 B; cf. also Gregory of Nazianzus CI 176 A; Chrysostom XCI 656, CLXIII 707, CCXXI 732, CCXXXIX 745; Isidorus II 33, 477 C; Firmus X 1489 B; Cyril of Alexandria LIV 289 B; Theodoret XIX 1197 B, LXII 1233 B, CVIII 1301 B.

There are also instances of its being addressed to communities of monks: καὶ ταῦτα ἀπέστειλα τῇ ὑμετέρᾳ θεοσεβείᾳ, Athanasius 25 695 A; ταῦτα καὶ ὅσα τοιαῦτα παρακαλῶ τὴν ὑμετέραν θεοσέβειαν βοᾶν πρὸς τὸν τῶν ὅλων Θεόν, Theodoret CLI 1432 D; cf. also Basil XXIII [7] 101 D, 102 B; Cyril of Alexandria XIX 125 C, XXVI 141 B; Theodoret CLI 1421 D.

Theodoret gives the title to deaconesses: περιττὸν δὲ οἶμαι συλλέγειν ταῦτα καὶ τῇ σῇ προσφέρειν θεοσεβείᾳ, XVII 1196 B, 1196 C, 1196 D, CI 1293 D.

In the following instances, θεοσέβεια refers to bodies of clergy: παρακαλῶ τοίνυν τὴν ὑμετέραν θεοσέβειαν νῦν πλείονα τῆς ποίμνης ποιήσασθαι προμήθειαν, Theodoret LXXV 1244 C; cf. also John of Antioch VII 1448 B; Cyril of Alexandria XXIII 133 D, 136 B; Theodoret LXXV 1244 B. It also refers to churches; that is, to Christian communities, clergy and faithful: πρὸς τὴν προσφιλεστάτην ὑμῶν θεοσέβειαν ὁ δεσπότης ἡμῶν Κωνσταντῖνος ὁ σεβαστὸς ὁ ἐμὸς πατήρ, letter of Constantine quoted in Athanasius 25 405 C; cf. also Athanasius 25 345 B, the letter of Pope Julius; Cyril of Alexandria XXIV 157 A, XXVIII 144 B.

---

[7] This letter is probably addressed to a community of monks although the superscription is παραθετικὴ πρὸς μονάζοντα; cf. Benedictine edition.

Athanasius has several examples addressed to the emperor: χρὴ γὰρ ἀπολογούμενόν με ἀληθεύειν τῇ σῇ θεοσεβείᾳ, *25* 600 C; also *25* 597 B, 601 A, 621 C, 625 A, 629 D, 637 B, and *26* 816 C.

The following examples are addressed to persons who are unidentified: Basil CCXIII 320 D; Cyril of Alexandria LXXVIII 361 C; Theodoret I 1173 B, II 1176 B, IV 1180 B, IX 1181 C, XXV 1205 B, XXXVIII 1216 C, LIV 1229 A, LXIII 1233 D, LXIV 1236 B; Procopius LXXII 2776 B.

θεοσεβέστατος: adj., *most godly;* as a substantive, *most godly Sir.*

The title θεοσεβέστατος is generally used in addressing bishops. There are a few instances of its use as a title for the emperor and for the lower clergy. It does not occur in Basil nor in Chrysostom, but it is a favorite title for bishops with Cyril of Alexandria. It is found as a title in papyri.[8]

The examples of θεοσεβέστατος addressed to bishops are as follows: τῇ χειροτονίᾳ τοῦ ὁσιωτάτου καὶ θεοσεβεστάτου τῆς Κωνσταντινουπολιτῶν ἁγίας Ἐκκλησίας ἐπισκόπου Μαξιμιανοῦ, John of Antioch III 165 A; οἵ τε κατὰ δύσιν καὶ ἀνατολὴν θεοσεβέστατοι ἐπίσκοποι, Cyril of Alexandria VIII 60 D; τὸν προειρημένον θεοσεβέστατον ἐπίσκοπον, Theodoret CLXX 1476 C. The following example indicates the conventional nature of the title: ᾔσθημεν τοίνυν τῇ συντυχίᾳ τοῦ μνημονευθέντος θεοσεβεστάτου ἀνδρός, Cyril of Alexandria XXXIX 176 A. For bishops, cf. also Gregory of Nazianzus CLXXI 280 C; Peter of Sebasteia, letter XXX 1 among the letters of Gregory of Nyssa; John of Antioch III 165 A, IV 173 B, V 248 A; Cyril of Alexandria VIII 60 B, XIII 96 B, 96 C, XVI 104 C, 104 D, XVII 108 A, 108 B, XVIII 124 C, XIX 128 A, XXIII 133 B, 136 A, 136 C, XXVIII 144 C, XXXVIII 168 C, 168 D, XL 184 A, 184 C, 185 A, 185 B, 185 C, 188 D, 189 B, 197 D, 200 C, XLII 221 B, 221 C, XLV 237 A, XLVIII 249 C, 252 A, 252 B, 252 C, 253 A, XLIX 253 D, L 276 C, LIV 288 B, 289 B, LV 316 C, LVI 320 B, LVIII 321 B, LXIII 328 B, 328 D, LXVII 336 A, LXXVII 360 C, LXXVIII 361 C, 364 A, 364 B, LXXIX 365 B; Theodoret LXXV 1244 B, LXXXV 1277 B, XCII 1285 C; Gennadius 1617 B.

[8] Moulton and Milligan s. v.; Preisigke s. v.

The emperor is addressed with θεοσεβέστατος as follows: θεοσεβέσ-τατε Αὔγουστε, Athanasius 25 612 B; τῷ θεοσεβεστάτῳ καὶ θεοφιλεστάτῳ βασιλεῖ, Cyril of Alexandria XLVIII 252 A; cf. also Athanasius 25 549 A; John of Antioch III 164 D, V 248 B.

The title is given to members of the lower clergy as follows: to archimandrites, οἱ θεοσεβέστατοι καὶ ἁγιώτατοι ἀρχιμανδρῖται, Cyril of Alexandria XXVIII 144 B; to priests, ὁ θεοσεβέστατος πρεσβύτερος Εὐσέβιος, Theodoret LX 1232 C, and also LXII 1233 B, LXXXVII 1281 B; to monks, Cyril of Alexandria XXVI 140 C and Theodoret LXXXVII 1281 A; to churches, Athanasius 25 344 C, Proclus II 856 B.

The following examples are addressed to persons whose station in life is not known: Nilus III 12, 573 B; Isidorus II 18, 469 B; Procopius XCVII 2792 D.

ὁσιότης: n., *Holiness.*

Ὁσιότης as a title for bishops is common. The instances of its being addressed to persons of other classes are very rare. It is used by all of the important authors except Synesius.

The passages in which ὁσιότης is addressed to bishops are as follows: τὴν δὲ σὴν ὁσιότητα παρακαλῶ μεμνῆσθαι τῶν ἐξ ἀρχῆς προτάσεων, Basil CXXVIII 219 A; καὶ εὐχέσθω σου ἡ ὁσιότης, John of Antioch V 249 A; οἶδεν ὑμῶν ἡ ὁσιότης, Cyril of Alexandria LXVII 336 D. Cf. also Athanasius 26 532 B; Basil XXX 110 C, XLVIII 141 E, LVII 151 B, LXI 155 D, LXVIII 161 B, XCVIII 191 D, CXX 212 A, CXLI 234 A and C, CLXIV 254 B, CXCVIII 290 A, CC 298 C, CCXXXIX 367 C, CCLXVIII 414 C; Gregory of Nazianzus LX 120 B, CCII 332 A; Gregory of Nyssa VI 11, XXV 15, XXX 1; Chrysostom CXII 669; Isidorus V 474, 1601 B; Firmus of Caesarea XXII 1497 C, XXIII 1497 C, XXXVII 1508 A, XXXVIII 1508 B, XLI 1509 B; Cyril of Alexandria XI 80 B, 85 B, XXXI 156 C, XXXIX 176 C, 180 B, 180 D, 181 B, 181 C, XL 201 A, XLI 201 B, XLII 221 B, XLV 228 D, 236 D, XLVI 240 A, XLVIII 249 C, 252 D, XLIX 253 C, 256 A, L 256 B, LVI 320 C, LXIII 328 C, LXIX 340 A, 340 D, LXXII 344 C, 345 A, 345 D, LXXVII 360 C; Alypius 148 C; Paul of Emesa 165 B, 165 D, 168 A; Atticus 349 B; John of Antioch I 1452 A,

1452 D, II 132 B, 132 C, III 165 A, IV 173 B, V 248 A,
249 A, VI 1461 D; Theodoret XI 1184 C, XVI 1192 C, XXIV
1205 A, XXXII 1209 D, 1212 A, XXXV 1212 D, XXXVI 1213 B,
1213 C, XLVII 1224 D, XLIX 1225 C, LII 1228 C, LIII 1228 D,
LX 1232 C, LXXVII 1248 A, 1252 A, LXXXIII 1268 B, 1268 C,
1273 B, LXXXV 1277 A, 1277 B, LXXXVI 1280 D, LXXXVII
1281 B, 1281 C, CII 1296 A, CIII 1296 D, CIX 1304 A, 1304 B,
1304 C, CX 1305 D, CXII 1309 A, 1309 D, CXIII 1513 C, 1317 C,
CXVI 1325 B, CXVII [9] 1325 D, CXXIII 1333 C, 1333 D, CXXVI
1337 D, CXXX 1348 C, CXXXII 1549 C, 1349 D, CXLVII 1409 A,
1412 A, 1412 C, CLXX 1476 B, 1476 C, 1481 B, 1481 C, 1481 D;
Gennadius 1617 C. Theodoret addresses ὁσιότης to Renatus, papal
representative to the Council of Ephesus: καὶ ταῦτα ἔδρασέ σου ἡ
ὁσιότης, CXVI 1324 C; also CXVIII 1328 B.

'Οσιότης also occurs in the following instances: to the emperor, οἱ καὶ
τὴν σὴν ἀναδιδάξουσιν ὁσιότητα, Athanasius 26 700 A and also 700 B; to
a priest, εὐξάσθω τοίνυν ἡ ὁσιότης σου τὴν περὶ ἡμῶν δόξαν ἐμπεδωθῆναι τῇ
ἀληθείᾳ, Theodoret XX 1197 C and also Nilus II 215, 312 D; to an
archimandrite, μονάζουσιν, οἳ παρὰ τῆς σῆς ὁσιότητος ἑτέρων ἕνεκα χρειῶν
ἀπεστάλησαν, Theodoret CXLI 1365 C; to a monk, ἐχρῆν μὲν τὴν σὴν
ὁσιότητα, ὦ μισοπονηρίας ἱερὸν τέμενος, σιωπῇ παραδοῦναι τὰ λήθης ἄξια καὶ
βαθείας σιγῆς, Isidorus III 178, 869 A; to the clergy, ὅτε ἐνέτυχον τοῖς
γράμμασι τῆς ὁσιότητος ὑμῶν, ὅσον ἐστέναξα καὶ ὠδυράμην, Basil CCXLVII
383 C; to a woman, καὶ τὴν σὴν παρακαλῶ ὁσιότητα ταῦτα δὴ λογίζεσθαι,
Theodoret LXIX 1237 D; to unknown persons, Basil CCXIII
320 B, Theodoret I 1173 B.

ὁσιώτατος: adj., *most holy*; as a substantive, *most holy Sir*.

The title ὁσιώτατος is used in referring to bishops. It occurs
frequently in Cyril of Alexandria and Theodoret, but only once in
Basil and John Chrysostom. We have found no examples in
Athanasius, Gregory of Nazianzus, and Gregory of Nyssa. Preisigke
records its use as a title in papyri.

The examples of its application to bishops are as follows: τῷ
ὁσιωτάτῳ καὶ ἁγιωτάτῳ δεσπότῃ ἐμῷ, ἀρχιεπισκόπῳ πατρὶ Μαξιμιανῷ, Cyril
of Alexandria XLIX 253 B; τῷ ὁσιωτάτῳ καὶ θεοφιλεστάτῳ συλλειτουργῷ

---

[9] Cf. page 2, footnote 2.

Δόμνῳ, Πρόκλος, ἐν Κυρίῳ χαίρειν, Proclus XIII 881 A; ὁ ὁσιώτατος ἀρχιεπίσκοπος ὁ κύριος Δόμνος, Theodoret XCII 1285 D. Cf. also Basil XCII 183 C; Chrysostom I 536; Isidorus II 101, 545 A; Cyril of Alexandria XI 80 B, XVII 108 A, 108 B, XVIII 124 C, XIX 128 A, XL 184 C, 185 A, 188 C, 201 A, XLVIII 249 C, 252 A, 253 A, LV 316 C, LVI 320 B, LXVII 336 A, LXXII 345 C, 345 D, LXXVIII 361 C; Paul of Emesa 165 B, 165 C, 168 A; John of Antioch I 1450 A, II 132 C, III 164 B, 165 A, IV 173 B, VI 1460 C; Proclus XIII 884 D; Firmus XIII 1492 A; Theodoret XIV 1189 D, LII 1228 C, XCIII 1288 A, 1288 B, CXVIII 1328 B, CXLIV 1373 C, CLXX 1476 C.

In only one instance is ὁσιώτατος applied to a person other than a bishop. Theodoret addresses it to the ascetic, Jacob: ὁ ὁσιώτατος καὶ ἁγιώτατος ἄνθρωπος τοῦ Θεοῦ, ὁ κύριος Ἰάκωβος, XLII 1220 B.

Once it is addressed to a person who is unknown: Firmus XLIII 1512 B.

πάπας: n., *Pope.*

In the literature which we have examined, most of the examples of the title πάπας are addressed to the bishop of Alexandria. It is found once for Pope Julius: κυρίῳ μακαριωτάτῳ πάπᾳ Ἰουλίῳ Οὐρσάκιος καὶ Οὐάλης, quoted in Athanasius 25 353 B. The passages in which the title is given to the bishop of Alexandria are as follows: Ἄρειος ὁ διωκόμενος ὑπὸ Ἀλεξάνδρου τοῦ πάπα ἀδίκως, Arius quoted in Theodoret H. E. I 5, 1; μακαριώτατε πάπα, addressed to Athanasius in 25 373 A. Cf. also Arius 708 C, 709 B; letters quoted in Athanasius 25 364 A, 369 A, 372 B, 376 A, and 26 708 C, 709 A, 712 C, 808 B; Basil CCLVIII 394 B; Cyril of Alexandria XLIV 225 C, 228 C.

We have noted three instances of its use where the identification of the persons addressed is uncertain or unknown. It is conjectured that the Apollinarius to whom the title is given in Origen 85 D is a bishop: [10] σὺ τὸν καλὸν ἡμῶν πάπαν Ἀπολλινάριον ἄσπασαι. The person to whom St. Basil refers in CXX 212 B and CXXI 212 D is quite unknown.

πατήρ: n., *Father.*

The use of πατήρ as a title of respect for elders and superiors is

[10] Smith and Wace s. v.

classical. In the literature examined, we have found it used only for ecclesiastics, generally for the Pope, the bishops of Constantinople and especially of Alexandria, and also for very aged and respected bishops. Examples of its use for other ecclesiastics are rare. We have noted no examples in Gregory of Nyssa, Gregory of Nazianzus, and Theodoret.

The title is addressed to the Pope as follows: ἡ ἀνατολὴ πᾶσα σχεδόν, τιμώτατε πάτερ, . . . μεγάλῳ χειμῶνι καὶ κλύδωνι κατασείεται, Basil LXX [11] 163 D; cf. also Cyril of Alexandria XI 80 B.

The following are illustrations of πατήρ as a title for the bishops of Alexandria: πάτερ προσφιλέστατε, addressed to Athanasius in 25 624 C; ὁ θεοφιλέστατος πατὴρ Θεόφιλος, Synesius CV 1488 B.   Cf. also Basil LXVI 159 B, LXXXII 175 D and E, XC 181 B, CCIV 306 D; Synesius LXVII 1417 B, 1429 A, CV 1484 D; Cyril of Alexandria XXXIX 180 D, 181 B, XL 200 C, XLV 236 A; Atticus 349 B; Alypius 145 D, 148 B.

Further illustrations of its use in addressing bishops are as follows: to the bishop of Constantinople, τῷ ὁσιωτάτῳ καὶ ἁγιωτάτῳ δεσπότῃ ἐμῷ ἀρχιεπισκόπῳ πατρὶ Μαξιμιανῷ, Cyril of Alexandria XLIX 253 B; to aged and venerable bishops, Basil XCVIII 192 E, CXXVIII 219 D, Paul of Emesa 165 C, John of Antioch IV 172 A. Cf. also Athanasius 25 384 C.

Cyril of Alexandria uses the title in referring to monks: XIX 125 C, LV 289 D.

In the following instances πατήρ is addressed to persons who are not identified: Synesius LXXVI 1441 B, CXXIII 1504 B, CXXXIII 1521 C; Procopius XVIII 2733 D.

φιλοθεΐα: n., *God-loving Self.*

The title φιλοθεΐα is used especially for bishops. There are occasional examples to other members of the clergy. The title occurs chiefly in Theodoret.

The passages in which φιλοθεΐα is addressed to bishops are as follows: ἐπέστειλα εὐχόμενός σου τὴν φιλοθεΐαν ἀφιλονεικοτάτῃ γνώμῃ δέξασθαι, John of Antioch I 1457 A; τὴν δὲ σὴν φιλοθεΐαν παρακαλῶ,

---

[11] Editors agree that this letter is addressed to Pope Damasus.   Cf. Deferrari, Vol. II, p. 49.

Theodoret XVI 1192 D; cf. also John of Antioch I 1456 D and
Theodoret XII 1184 D, XVI 1193 B, XXIV 1204 D, XXXV
1213 A, XXXVI 1213 B, 1213 C, XLIX 1225 C, LII 1228 C,
LXXVII 1248 D, LXXXIV 1276 A, 1276 B, LXXXVII 1281 A,
CII 1296 C, CXIII 1313 C, CXXIII 1333 D, 1336 A, CXXXII
1349 C, CXXXV 1356 A, 1356 B.

Theodoret addresses the title to ecclesiastics with special func-
tions as follows: to Renatus, delegate of the Pope, πρὸς τὴν ὑμετέραν
φιλοθεΐαν ἀπέστειλα, CXVI 1325 C; to an oeconomus, τοὺς μὲν ὑπὲρ
τῆς εὐσεβείας ἀγῶνας τῆς σῆς φιλοθεΐας παρὰ πολλῶν μεμαθήκαμεν, CV
1300 C; to archimandrites, προσφέρω σου τῇ φιλοθεΐᾳ τὸν ἐμοὶ πανε-
πέραστον ἀσπασμὸν, CXXVII 1340 C and also CXXIX 1341 A,
CXLII 1368 A.

The remaining examples are as follows: to priests, οὐκ ἔλαθον οἱ
τῆς σῆς φιλοθεΐας ἀγῶνες, Theodoret CVII 1301 A, and also XXVIII
1208 A, LI 1228 A, CVIII 1301 B; to a monk, διὰ ταῦτα τῆς σῆς
φιλοθεΐας ἐξήρτημαι, Theodoret CXLIII 1368 D; to a deaconess, τὴν
σὴν διδάσκων φιλοθεΐαν ἄπερ φρονῶ, Theodoret CI 1293 D.

TITLES FOR THE CLERGY IN GENERAL

There are no titles reserved for the lower clergy as a whole, or
for special ranks within the lower clergy, with the exception of the
following very rare titles which are found addressed to deacons.[12]

γλυκύτης: n., *Sweetness.*

St. John Chrysostom is the only author who makes use of this
title. He uses it on only two occasions and both times he is addressing the deacon Theodotus: ἡμᾶς δὲ μετὰ τῶν ἐνταῦθα θορύβων, μᾶλλον
δὲ τῶν θανάτων τῶν καθημερινῶν, οὐχ ὡς ἔτυχε λυπεῖ καὶ τὸ τῆς σῆς
κεχωρίσθαι γλυκύτητος, καὶ τῆς γνησίας καὶ εἰλικρινοῦς διαθέσεως, LXVII
645; οὐ μικρὰν εἴχομεν παραμυθίαν . . . ἐπιστέλλειν σου τῇ γλυκύτητι,
CXL 696.

σπουδαιότατος: adj., *most zealous.*

St. Basil uses the title in referring to deacons, as follows:

---

[12] For titles which were addressed to special ranks of lower clergy, cf.
Index under *priests, deacons, subdeacons, lectors, archimandrites, monks,
chorepiscopi.*

ὁ ἀγαπητὸς καὶ σπουδαιότατος ἀδελφὸς ἡμῶν συνδιάκονος Ἐλπίδιος, CXXXVIII 229 B; cf. also LXXXIX 180 C, CXXXVIII 229 B, CXCVII 288 C.

It occurs once in the letter of Origen to his pupil, Gregory Thaumaturgus: κύριέ μου σπουδαιότατε καὶ αἰδεσιμώτατε υἱὲ Γρηγόριε, 88 A.

The titles which were given to clergymen of all ranks are as follows:

ἀγάπη: n., *Charity.*

The title is used most frequently in addressing bishops. There are examples of its being addressed to ecclesiastical bodies, such as churches or groups of clergy, and to monks and priests, but it is never addressed to deacons. The title is a favorite one with Basil and John Chrysostom. It is found rarely in the letters of Cyril of Alexandria, Gregory of Nyssa, Gregory of Nazianzus, Athanasius, Nilus, and Isidorus. There are no examples of its use in the letters of Theodoret and Synesius. Being a purely Christian word, it never occurs in the letters of the pagans, Julian and Libanius.

The beginnings of the use of ἀγάπη as a title are traceable in certain passages of early Christian literature. The following examples show how the quality came to be identified with the individual: ἁπλούστερον ὑμῖν γράφω, ἵνα συνιῆτε · ἔγω περίψημα τῆς ἀγάπης ὑμῶν, Pseudo-Barnabas VI 5; ἀσπάζεται ὑμᾶς ἡ ἀγάπη τῶν ἀδελφῶν τῶν ἐν Τρωάδι, Ignatius to the Philadelphians XI 2; cf. also Ignatius to the Trallians XIII 1, to the Romans IX 1, to the Smyrnians XII 1. In all these instances, the writer is addressing a church, that is, a congregation with its clergy. After the use of ἀγάπη as a title became conventional, it was still employed to address churches; for example, ταῦτα δὲ πρὸς τὴν ὑμετέραν ἐπεστείλαμεν ἀγάπην, Proclus II 872 D; cf. also Basil CXL 232 C, CCLI 386 B.

There are several examples of ἀγάπη as a title addressed to bodies of clergy whose members were of different orders, generally of lower clergy: καθάπερ ὑμῶν παρεκάλεσα τὴν ἀγάπην, Chrysostom CXXIII 678; οἶμαι δὲ τὴν ἀγάπην ὑμῶν καὶ ἐντυχεῖν τῷ βιβλίῳ, ὃ περὶ τούτων αὐτῶν συγγεγράφαμεν, Cyril of Alexandria LV 296 A; cf. also Athanasius 25 312 D, Basil CCLVI 391 B, Chrysostom CLXXIV 711, Cyril of Alexandria LV 292 A.

Bishops are addressed with ἀγάπη as follows: τὸ δὲ καθέκαστον αὐτὸς ὁ προειρημένος συνδιάκονος ἀναγγελεῖ ὑμῶν τῇ ἀγάπῃ, Basil XC 182 C; προσαγορεύομεν ὑμῶν τὴν ἀγάπην, Chrysostom CLVII 704; Κύριλλος ἀσπαζόμενος ἐν Κυρίῳ τὴν ὑμετέραν ἀγάπην, Cyril of Alexandria LXXXV 377 A. Cf. also Athanasius 25 320 B, 356 A; Basil LI 143 B, LIX 153 B, LXV 157 E, LXXXI [13] 173 E, XCII 183 E, C 195 E, CXIX 210 C, CXXXII 225 A, CCIII 300 A and C, CCV 308 A, CCXVII 325 A, CCXVIII 331 B, CCXXXI 354 B, CCXLII 371 D, CCXLIII 373 A, 374 C, CCXLIV 381 B, CCXLV 382 C, CCXLVIII 384 B, CCLV 390 A, CCLXV 408 D, CCLXVI 411 E, CCLXVII 413 D; Gregory of Nazianzus XLII [14] 88 A; Amphilochius 93 B, 93 C, 97 A; Chrysostom I 530, 532, XXXVII 631, LXXXVII 654, CLXII 706, CLXIII 706, CLXVI 708; Cyril of Alexandria LXXXV 377 A, 377 B; Nestorius 49 B, 52 C.

To a chorepiscopus: τοῖς δὲ ἀποσταλεῖσι παρὰ τῆς ἀγάπης σου ὑπερήσθην, οἷς ὑπῆρχε μὲν ἡδίστος εἶναι, καὶ κατὰ τὴν ἑαυτῶν φύσιν, Basil CCXCI 430 D.

The title is given to priests in the following instances: ἡμεῖς δὲ ταύτην ὑπὲρ ἑαυτῶν τὴν ἀπολογίαν πρὸς τὴν ἀγάπην ὑμῶν ποιούμεθα, Gregory of Nyssa XVII 2; ἠρώτησέ με, ἡ ὑμετέρα ἀγάπη, τί ἐστιν, ὅπερ φάσκει πρὸς τὸν Θεὸν ὁ Βαρούχ, Nilus II 33, 213 A; cf. also Chrysostom XXII 624, LIII 638, CCXLI 746.

Ἀγάπη is used as a title for monks as follows: καὶ γράμμασι προσομιλεῖν τῇ ἀγάπῃ ἡμῶν, Basil CCXXVI 346 A; παρακαλῶ αὐτοὺς διὰ τῆς σῆς ἀγάπης, Basil CCLXII 404 A; cf. also Basil CCLXII 404 C, Chrysostom CCVII 727. It occurs in a letter to the monk Caesarius among the spuria of Chrysostom, 760.[15]

There are two examples which cannot be classified. One occurs in a letter addressed to Theodora, a canoness: ὀκνηροὺς ἡμᾶς ποιεῖ πρὸς τὸ γράφειν τὸ μὴ πεπεῖσθαι τὰς ἐπιστολὰς ἡμῶν πάντως ἐγχειρίζεσθαι τῇ σῇ

---

[13] This letter is ascribed by Wittig to St. John Chrysostom; cf. Deferrari, Vol. II, p. 91.

[14] This letter is found among the letters of St. Basil as letter XLVII, but critics ascribe it to St. Gregory. It is interesting, however, that this is the only clear example of the use of ἀγάπη as a title in the letters of St. Gregory.

[15] The letter is dated about 450.

ἀγάπη, Basil CLXXIII 260 E. The other is addressed to a layman of high rank: ἂν γὰρ δεξώμεθα ἐπιστολὴν τῆς ἀγάπης σου, τὰ περὶ τῆς ῥώσεως ἡμῖν ἀπαγγέλλουσαν τῆς σῆς, καὶ τῶν σοὶ προσηκόντων ἁπάντων, πολλήν, καὶ ἐν ἀλλοτρίᾳ διατρίβοντες γῇ, δεξόμεθα παράκλησιν, Chrysostom CCV 726.

The following examples are addressed to persons who are unidentified: Basil CXIV 207 A; Gregory of Nyssa XIX 3; Chrysostom XXXV 630, LXIII 644, CLXXXIX 718; Cyril of Alexandria IX 61 A; Isidorus I 459, 433 D.

In several cases it is difficult to determine whether ἀγάπη should be regarded as a title or taken literally; for example, Chrysostom XXII 625, XXIII 625; XLII 633, LXX 647, CXII 668, CXCIV 720, CCXVIII 731, CCXXXII 739.

St. Basil has a peculiar use of the expression ἡ ἐν Χριστῷ ἀγάπη, probably as a title of special esteem. It occurs four times, twice to a bishop and twice to a community of monks: to St. Ambrose, bishop of Milan, γνωρίζομεν δέ σου τῇ ἐν Χριστῷ ἀγάπῃ, ὅτι . . . , CXCVII 288 C; to Ascholius, bishop of Thessalonica,[16] δευτέρας εὐχῆς ἄξιον γράμμασι συνεχέσι τῆς ἐν Χριστῷ σου ἀγάπης τρέφεσθαι τὴν ψυχήν, CLXV 256 A; to monks, ὃ τοίνυν ἐγὼ μεθ' ὑμῶν ἠβουλήθην ποιῆσαι, ἡ ἐν Χριστῷ ὑμῶν ἀγάπη καὶ δίχα μου ποιησάτω, XXIII [17] 102 C; τούτου ἕνεκεν ἐπειράθην ἐπιστεῖλαι ὑμῖν, παρακαλῶν τὴν ἐν Χριστῷ ἀγάπην ὑμῶν, ὥστε τὰς ἐξ ἑνὸς μέρους γινομένας διαβολὰς μὴ πάντη παραδέχεσθαι ὡς ἀληθεῖς, CCXXVI 346 C.

ἀγαπητός: adj., *beloved;* as a substantive, *beloved.*

The title ἀγαπητός is usually addressed to all classes of ecclesiastics and to churches. It occurs most frequently for bishops. Until the end of the third century, however, it seems to have been applied to any fellow Christian.

The first examples of ἀγαπητός as a term of both direct and indirect address are found in the Epistles of the New Testament. It is a direct title in the following instances: διόπερ, ἀγαπητοί μου, φεύγετε

---

[16] The Benedictine editors are of the opinion that this letter was addressed to Soranus, dux of Scythia, but the presence of the titles θεοσέβεια and σύνεσις and the above title point to the conclusion that the superscription as we have it is correct.

[17] Cf. p. 8, footnote 7.

ἀπὸ τῆς εἰδωλολατρίας, I Cor. X 14; ἀγαπητέ, μὴ μιμοῦ τὸ κακὸν ἀλλὰ τὸ ἀγαθόν, III John 11. Cf. also Rom. XI 28, XII 19, II Cor. VII 1, XII 19, Philip. II 12, Heb. VI 9, I Pet. II 11, IV 12, III 1; II Pet. III 8, 14, 17; III John 2, 5; Jude 3, 17, 20. Passages in which it is used in indirect address are as follows: Φιλήμονι τῷ ἀγαπητῷ καὶ συνεργῷ, Philem. 1; καθὼς καὶ ὁ ἀγαπητὸς ἡμῶν ἀδελφὸς Παῦλος κατὰ τὴν αὐτῷ δοθεῖσαν σοφίαν ἔγραψεν ὑμῖν, II Pet. III 15. Cf. also Rom. I 7, XVI 5, 8, 9; I Cor. IV, 14, 17, XV 58; Eph. V 1, VI 21; Philip. IV 1; Col. I 7, IV 7, 9, 14; II Tim. I 2; Philem. 16; III John 1. Contrary to the usage of later times, St. Paul addresses it once to a woman: ἀσπάσασθε Περσίδα τὴν ἀγαπητήν, Rom. XVI 12.

'Αγαπητός is found in the early Christian writers, usually in direct address to churches; for example, ὁρᾶτε, ἀγαπητοί, ὅτι οὐ μόνον πίστις ἀλλὰ προφητεία ἐν τῇ γυναικὶ γέγονεν, I Clement XII 8; ταῦτα δὲ παραινῶ ὑμῖν, ἀγαπητοί, εἰδῶς, ὅτι καὶ ὑμεῖς οὕτως ἔχετε, Ignatius to the Smyrnians IV 1. Cf. also Ignatius to the Magnesians XI 2; I Clement I 1, VII 1, XVI 17, XXI 1, XXIV 1, XXXV 5, et passim. Ignatius has the following example to an individual: ἀσπάζομαι Ἄτταλον τὸν ἀγαπητόν μου, to Polycarp VIII 2.

From the end of the third century, ἀγαπητός was used only in addressing clergymen and churches. Theodoret is the only important author who does not employ it. Athanasius uses it most frequently; Gregory of Nyssa, but once.

The examples are as follows:

To bishops: ἐρρῶσθαι ὑμᾶς ἐν Κυρίῳ εὔχομαι, ἀγαπητοί, Alexander of Alexandria I 572 A; κυρίῳ μου ἀγαπητῷ ἀδελφῷ καὶ ποθεινοτάτῳ συλλειτουργῷ Ἐπικτήτῳ, Ἀθανάσιος ἐν Κυρίῳ χαίρειν, Athanasius 26 1049 A; ἐρρῶσθαί σε ἐν Κυρίῳ, ἀγαπητὲ καὶ ποθεινότατε ἀδελφέ, Theophilus 61 C. Cf. also Dionysius of Alexandria 1272 B, 1288 C; Alexander of Alexandria I 552 A, 560 C, 564 A, 569 C, II 572 A; 577 B; Eusebius of Caesarea, letter to Flacillus, in H. E. IV; Athanasius 25 221 A, 236 D, 252 B, 253 B, 277 D, 280 B, 285 C, 288 A, 289 C, 289 D, 292 C, 308 C, 312 A, 313 D, 317 C, 321 A, 321 B, 324 B, 325 A, 328 A, 332 C, 333 C, 336 B, 337 A, 356 A, 372 A, 372 B, 384 B, 524 A, 525 A, 528 A, 529 B, 529 C, 532 C, and 26 529 A,

648 C, 796 A, 796 B, 797 A, 1029 A, 1032 B, 1033 B, 1045 C, 1069 B, 1073 A, 1080 C, 1084 B, 1168 C; Peter II of Alexandria, quoted in Theodoret H. E. IV 22, 27; Theophilus 61 B, 61 C; Basil CCXLII 372 C, CCLXIII 405 A; Gregory of Nazianzus CII 196 B; Celestine of Rome 89 B, 92 A; Cyril of Alexandria XXIX 144 D, XXXIX 173 C, XL 181 D, XLVIII 249 B, LXXVII 360 B, LXXXIII 1077 B.

To priests: ἐρρῶσθαι ὑμᾶς ἐν Κυρίῳ εὔχομαι, ἀγαπητοὶ καὶ ποθεινότατοι υἱοί, Athanasius 26 1168 B; τὸν εὐλαβέστατον καὶ ἀγαπητὸν ἀδελφὸν ἡμῶν Δωρόθεον τὸν συμπρεσβύτερον, Basil CCXLIII 376 A. Cf. also Athanasius 25 312 C and 26 1165 C, 1168 B, 1168 D, 1169 A; Basil CCV 308 A; Gregory of Nazianzus LXXXV 157 B; Chrysostom to Innocent 535; Cyril of Alexandria XXXVII 168 C, LIV 289 C.

To deacons: μέχρι τῆς ἐπιδημίας τοῦ ἀγαπητοῦ ἀδελφοῦ ἡμῶν Λιβανίου τοῦ συνδιακόνου, Basil CCLXVIII 414 D; μὴ τοίνυν κάμῃς, ἀγαπητέ, Chrysostom CCVI 726. Cf. also Athanasius 25 368 A; Basil LXVII 160 C, CXXXVI 228 A, CXXXVIII 229 B; Gregory of Nazianzus XLII [18] 88 B, CCXXVIII 372 B; Chrysostom to Innocent of Rome, 530; Cyril of Alexandria XI 85 B, XIII 96 C; Alypius 148 C.

To monks: ὑμεῖς δέ, ἀγαπητοί, δέξασθε ταῦτα, Athanasius 25 695 B; ἔμαθον παρὰ τοῦ ἀγαπητοῦ μονάζοντος Παύλου ὅτι . . , Cyril of Alexandria LVII 320 C. Cf. also Athanasius 25 692 A and 26 977 C, 980 A, 980 B, 980 C, 1172 A, 1185 A, 1188 B; Serapion 925 C; Basil CCLVIII 393 C; Cyril of Alexandria XIX 128 C, XXVI 140 C, 141 B, LVIII 321 B; also the letter to the monk Caesarius among the spuria of Chrysostom, 760.[19]

For groups of clergy of different ranks: Ἀλέξανδρος, πρεσβυτέροις καὶ διακόνοις Ἀλεξανδρείας καὶ Μαρεώτου, παρὼν παροῦσιν, ἀγαπητοῖς ἀδελφοῖς ἐν Κυρίῳ χαίρειν, Alexander of Alexandria III 581 C; τοὺς ἀγαπητούς, τὸν εὐλαβέστατον πρεσβύτερον Ἰωάννην, καὶ τὸν τιμιώτατον διάκονον Παῦλον, Chrysostom CLXVIII 709. Cf. also Athanasius 25 349 A, Cyril of Alexandria I 9 A, XXIII 132 D, LV 289 C.

---

[18] Letter XLII is found also among the letters of St. Basil as number XLVII.
[19] The letter is dated about 450.

To churches: ἀγαπητοὶ ἀδελφοί, Athanasius 25 360 B; τοῖς ἀγαπη-τοῖς καὶ ποθεινοτάτοις ἀδελφοῖς πρεσβυτέροις, διακόνοις, καὶ λαῷ Κωνσταν-τινουπόλεως, Cyril of Alexandria XVIII 124 A. Cf. also Eusebius, quoted in Theodoret H. E. I 12, 18; Athanasius 25 344 B, 345 A, 348 A, 352 A, 361 D, 408 A; Basil CCLI 388 A; Cyril of Alexan-dria XX 128 D, 129 B, 129 C, XXI 132 A, XXIV 137 A, 137 C, 137 D.

To persons who are unidentified: Origen to Africanus [20] 48 B; Athanasius 25 325 B, 373 B, 420 A, 476 B, 1085 A, 1168 C; Basil CCLXXXV 425 C; Gregory of Nazianzus XCVI 169 B, CCXXIII 364 C; Gregory of Nyssa II 18; Firmus XXVII 1501 A; Nilus IV 1, 549 D, and 40, 569 B; Isidorus I 475, 441 B.

ἀγχίνοια: n., *Sagacity*.

The title ἀγχίνοια occurs but rarely in the literature examined. Three times it is addressed to members of the clergy and once to a person who is not identified. The passages are as follows: to Eustathius, bishop of Sebaste, ὅπερ δ' ἂν κατηγορήσωσιν ἡμῶν, ἐκεῖνο παρὰ τῆς σῆς ἀγχινοίας ἐξεταζέσθωσαν, Basil CXIX 211 A; to Acacius, bishop, ἀναγκαίως ἐκεῖνό φημι, τῆς σῆς ἀγχινοίας ἀποχρώντως ἐχούσης τὸ εὐμαθές, Cyril of Alexandria XLI 201 C; to Diodorus, priest, ἐκεῖνο γὰρ πάντως συνειδέ σου ἡ ἀγχίνοια, ὅτι . . Basil CXXXV 226 C; to Agapetus, who is unidentified, οὕτω γὰρ καὶ ἡμεῖς χάριν πολλὴν ὁμολο-γήσομεν τῇ ἀγχινοίᾳ [21] τῇ σῇ, Chrysostom CLXXV 712.

εὐλάβεια: n., *Piety*.

Εὐλάβεια is one of the most common titles of address. It is ap-plied to the clergy in general and to bishops in particular. There are very rare instances of its use in addressing lay persons, both men and women. It is found commonly in Athanasius, Basil, Gregory of Nazianzus, John Chrysostom, and Cyril of Alexandria. It appears occasionally in Theodoret and only once in Gregory of Nyssa. There are no examples in Isidorus, Nilus, and Synesius, nor in the pagans, Julian and Libanius. It is recorded as a title in papyri.[22]

---

[20] It is uncertain whether Africanus was a clergyman or not.

[21] Omnes mss. ὁμολογήσομεν τῇ εὐγενείᾳ, (Migne Edition).

[22] Moulton and Milligan s. v.; Preisigke s. v.

The title is addressed to bishops as follows: ἀπέστειλα τῇ σῇ εὐλαβείᾳ, Athanasius 26 605 C; ἐπειδὴ δὲ ᾐτήσαμεν ἡμεῖς μαρτυρίαν τῆς σῆς εὐλαβείας καὶ τῶν λοιπῶν ἐπισκόπων, καταφρονήσας ἡμῶν πρὸς Ἄνθιμον ᾤχετο, Basil CXXI 212 E; ἡδὺ μὲν καὶ ἄλλως τὸ προσαγορεύειν τὴν σὴν εὐλάβειαν, Gregory of Nazianzus CXXVII 221 B. Cf. also Alexander of Alexandria I 548 A; Theophilus 61 B; Athanasius 25 224 B, 277 D, 388 B, 524 B, 525 B, 685 A, and 26 625 A, 637 A, 1069 B, 1073 B, 1073 C, 1080 C, 1180 B, 1182 A; Basil XLIX 142 B, LX 155 C, CXVII 209 C, CXIX 210 D, CXX 212 A, CXXI 212 D, CXXII 213 C, CXXX 222 A, CXXXII 224 E, CLXI 252 E, CLXIX 258 B, 259 B, CLXXXI 265 C, CLXXXIV 266 D, CXC 283 A, 283 D, CXCI 284 A, CXCV 286 E, 287 A, CXCVII 288 C, CXCVIII 289 D, 290 A, CXCIX 290 C, 291 A, CC 297 E, 298 B, CCIII 300 D, CCXVII 324 D, CCXXXI 354 C, CCXLIII 375 A, CCXLVIII 384 A, CCLV 390 A, 390 B, CCLX 395 D, CCLXIII 407 D, CCLXIV 407 E, 408 B, CCLXV 409 A, 410 D, 411 C, CCLXVI 413 A, CCLXVII 413 E, CCCLXI [23] 463 E, CCCLXIII [23] 465 C; Gregory of Nazianzus XVI 49 C, XVII 52 B, XVIII 52 C, LXXVII 141 C, CXV 212 C, CXXXVIII 233 B, CXXXIX 236 B, CLII 257 B, 257 C, CLIX 265 C, 268 A, CLX 268 A, CLXII 268 C, 269 A, CLXIII 269 C, CLXIII 272 A, CLXXXIII 297 B, CLXXXV 304 B, CCXLII 384 C; Amphilochus 93 B; Chrysostom to Innocent 529, 535, also XXV 626, XXVII 626, 627, XXX 628, LXXXV 653, LXXXVI 653, LXXXVII 654, LXXXVIII 654, 655, XC 655, CVIII 667, CX 668, CXII 668, CXIV 670, CXXXI 690, CXLII 696, CXLIX 700, CL 701, CLIII 702, CLVII 704, CLVIII 704, CLXII 706, CLXVI 708, CLXVII 709, CLXXXI 714, CC 723, CCXXX 737, CCXXXIII 739, CCXXXV 740; Cyril of Alexandria XIII 96 A, 96 B, XVII 108 B, 108 C, 120 B, LXXVI 353 D, 356 A; Celestine of Rome 92 A; John of Antioch I 1453 A, VI 1461 A; Nestorius 44 A.

The title is given to a chorepiscopus: ἡ εὐλάβειά σου ἀφ' ἡμῶν δέεται προστασίας, Firmus V 1485 A; and to archimandrites, ἡ σὴ εὐλάβεια γνώσεται, Cyril of Alexandria LVIII 521 B.

Εὐλάβεια occurs much less frequently as a title for priests. Examples are as follows: διὰ τοῦτο ἐγράψαμεν τῇ σῇ εὐλαβείᾳ, Gregory

---

[23] Letters CCCLXI and CCCLXIII are considered unauthentic.

of Nazianzus CII 193 B; ἐπεστάλκαμέν σου τῇ εὐλαβείᾳ, letter of Constantius among the letters of Chrysostom, 746; ἀπολογείσθω τοίνυν ἡ σὴ εὐλάβεια τοῖς ἔτερα ἀνθ᾽ ἑτέρων ἐκεῖσε λαλοῦσι, Cyril of Alexandria LIV 289 C. Cf. also Athanasius 26 1168 B; Basil CLVI 246 C, CCXXIV 342 B, CCXL 369 B, CCXXXVIII 366 C; Gregory of Nazianzus XL 84 A, CII 193 B; Gregory of Nyssa XVII 3; Chrysostom XXII 625, XXIII 625, XXVIII 627, LIV 638, LXVI 644, LXXVIII 650, XCI 656, CI 662, CXIX 674, CLXXX 714, CCXXI 733, CCXXV 735, CLXI 706; Cyril of Alexandria LIV 288 A, 289 B.

Chrysostom addresses εὐλάβεια to a deacon: τὸν κύριόν μου τὸν τιμιώτατον τὸν ἀναγνώστην Θεόδοτον παρακατατίθεμαί σου τῇ εὐλάβεια, CXXXV 693.

Chrysostom also uses it in referring to monks: τὴν διάθεσιν, ἣν ἔχομεν πρὸς τὴν εὐλάβειαν τὴν ὑμετέραν, LVI 640; cf. also XXXVI 630, LV 639, LVI 640.

The following examples are addressed to groups of clergy of various ranks: καὶ τοῦ παντὸς κλήρου τὸ πλήρωμα διὰ τῆς ὑμετέρας εὐλαβείας κατασπαζόμεθα, Basil CCXIX 333 B; ἔγνω που πάντως ὑμῶν ἡ εὐλάβεια τὰ ἀθέσμως, John of Antioch, among the letters of Theodoret 1448 A; cf. also Basil CCXXVII 351 B and CCXLVI 383 D, John of Antioch 1448 B, Cyril of Alexandria LV 293 C, Theodoret LXXV 1244 B.

The title is used to address churches: . . . ἐπιστολῆς, ἧς πρὸς τὴν ὑμετέραν εὐλάβειαν διεπεμψάμεθα, Athanasius 26 720 A; διὰ τοῦ γράμματος τὴν εὐλάβειαν ὑμῶν ἐπισκεπτόμεθα, Basil LXII 156 B. Cf. also Athanasius 25 312 A; Basil CCXX 333 C, CCXXI 334 B, CCXXII 334 D.

We have found the following examples of εὐλάβεια as a title for religious women: for the canonicae, ἃ μὲν οὖν ἤκουσα ἐπιζητεῖσθαι παρὰ τῆς εὐλαβείας ὑμῶν, ταῦτά ἐστιν, Basil LII 146 D and also 144 E; for the head of a religious community, ὥρμησα μὲν καὶ αὐτὸς πρὸς τὴν σὴν εὐλάβειαν, Gregory of Nazianzus CCXXII 361 C, and CCXXIII 364 C, 368 A; for deaconesses, ἐπιστέλλω σου τῇ εὐλαβείᾳ ἀπὸ Καισαρείας αὐτῆς, Chrysostom XII 609 and III 572, 589, VI 598, XI 609, XIII 610, XIV 616, 618, XVII 621, XCIV 658, CIII 663, CLXXXV 716.

Athanasius gives the title to the emperor: μαρτυρῆσαι τῇ σῇ εὐλαβείᾳ, 25 596 A; cf. also 25 597 A, 597 C, and 26 816 C.

As a title for laymen, εὐλάβεια occurs very rarely: τὴν ὀφειλομένην πρόσρησιν ἀποδιδόαμέν σου τῇ εὐλαβείᾳ, Chrysostom CCXVI 730; cf. also Chrysostom XLVI 634. For laywomen, there are the following examples: τούτου χάριν γεγράφαμέν σου τῇ εὐλαβείᾳ, letter of Constantius in the corpus of Chrysostom, 743; cf. also Chrysostom LII 637, CXXXIII 692, CCXXIX 737, CCXXXI 737. Basil has the following example to Eupaterius and his daughter: ταῦτα, ὥσπερ ἐν κεφαλαίῳ, ἀρκούντως τῇ εὐλαβείᾳ ὑμῶν εἰρήσθω, CLIX 248 D.

In the following instances εὐλάβεια is addressed to persons whose station in life is uncertain or unknown: Basil LXXI 164 D, CCXLIX 384 D; Gregory of Nazianzus LVIII 113 A, LX 120 A, LXXXIV 157 B; Chrysostom XXI 624, LXIII 643, CXCVI 721; Cyril of Alexandria VIII 60 B, LXXX 365 C; Theodoret VI 1180 C, XXVI 1205 C, XXXIX 1216 C, LVI 1229 B.

εὐλαβέστατος: adj., *most pious.*

Εὐλαβέστατος is very common as a title for the clergy, especially for bishops and priests. There are rare examples of its application to the emperor and to lay people, chiefly women. The term occurs in all the important authors of the fourth and fifth centuries, except Isidorus and Nilus. Milligan records the title as common for clergy after the close of the close of the fifth century.

Chrysostom, Synesius, and Cyril of Alexandria use εὐλαβέστατος frequently as a title for bishops; for example, καὶ γὰρ εὐθέως ἀπέστειλα τὸν κύριόν μου τὸν εὐλαβέστατον πρεσβύτερον τὸν Τερέντιον πρὸς τὸν κύριόν μου τὸν εὐλαβέστατον ἐπίσκοπον Ὀτρήϊον τὸν Ἀραβισσοῦ, Chrysostom CXXVI 687; τοῖς εὐλαβεστάτοις ἐπισκόποις Διοσκόρῳ καὶ Παύλῳ τὸ περιμάχητον ἦν, Synesius LXVII 1420 A; ἐρρῶσθαί σε, καὶ μνημονεύειν ἡμῶν, τῷ Κυρίῳ εὔχομαι, εὐλαβέστατε καὶ θεοφιλέστατε ἀδελφέ, Cyril of Alexandria XXXI 156 D. Cf. also Chrysostom to Innocent 529, 534, 535, and XXV 626, LXXXVII 654, LXXXVIII 655, CIX 667, CXXXI 690, CXLII 696, CLII 701, CLXVI 708, CLXXXIV 716; Synesius LXVII 1412 B, 1420 B, 1421 C, 1421 D, 1424 A, 1441 C; Cyril of Alexandria II 40 C, 41 A, IV 44 C, XI 81 B, 84 B, XIV 97 A, XVI 104 A, 104 C, 104 D, XVII 105 C, XVIII 124 A, XIX 125 D, XXIII 133 C, 133 D, 136 B, XXXI 149 D,

XXXVII 168 C, 168 D, 169 B, XL 184 A, 185 A, 185 C, 197 D, 200 D, 201 A, XLV 237 A, XLVIII 249 B, 252 A, 252 B, 252 C, 252 D, 253 A, 253 D, LIV 288 B, LVII 321 A, LVIII 321 B, 321 C, LXXVI 357 A, 357 B, 360 B, LXXXIV 385 B; Nestorius 49 B; Maximianus 148 D; Atticus 349 D; John of Antioch VI 1460 C. Theodoret addresses the title once to chorepiscopi: τῶν εὐλαβεστάτων καὶ θεοφιλεστάτων πρεσβυτέρων Ὑπατίου καὶ Ἀβραμίου τῶν χωρεπισκόπων, CXIII 1317 C.

Archimandrites are given the title as follows: ὁ εὐλαβέστατος διάκονος καὶ ἀρχιμανδρίτης Μάξιμος, Cyril of Alexandria LXX 341 B; cf. also LXIX 337 D, 340 C.

Εὐλαβέστατος appears as a title for priests in the letters of Basil, Chrysostom, and Theodoret, and in a few minor writers; for example, ἔδωκα τὴν ἐπιστολὴν προθύμως τῷ ποθεινοτάτῳ καὶ εὐλαβεστάτῳ ἀδελφῷ Σαγκτισσίμῳ τῷ συμπρεσβυτέρῳ, Basil CXXXII 225 A; ταῦτ' οὖν εἰδότες, κύριοί μου τιμιώτατοι καὶ εὐλαβέστατοι, μὴ διαλίπητε διηνεκῶς, Chrysostom XXII 624; ὁ εὐλαβέστατος πρεσβύτερος Πέτρος, Theodoret CXIV 1324 A. Cf. also Basil CLVI 246 B, CXCVII 288 E, CCIII 302 D, CCXX 333 C, CCXXVI 346 A, CCXXXIX 367 C, CCXLIII 376 A, CCXLV 382 D, CCLIII 389 B, CCLIV 389 D, CCLV 390 B, CCLVI 390 C, 391 A, CCLXVIII 414 E; Chrysostom XIII 611, XXII 625, XXIII 625, LIII 637, LIV 639, LX 642, LXII 643, LXXVIII 650, LXXIX 651, CXIV 671, CXXIII 677, 678, CXXVI 686, 687, CXLVIII 700, CLV 703, CLVI 703, CLVII 704, CLVIII 704, CLIX 705, CLX 705, CLXI 706, CLXII 706, CLXIII 707, CLXIV 707, CLXV 708, CLXVII 709, CLXVIII 709, CLXXV 711, CCXXI 733, CCXXIV 735; Nestorius 44 A, 44 B; Cyril of Alexandria LVIII 321 B, LXIII 328 C; Theodoret LXXVII 1252 B, LXXXVI 1277 C, CXV 1324 B, CXXXII 1349 D.

Εὐλαβέστατος occurs as a title for deacons in the following passages: καὶ ἀμειβόμεθά σε διὰ τοῦ αὐτοῦ ἀνδρὸς τοῦ εὐλαβεστάτου συνδιακόνου ἡμῶν καὶ ἀδελφοῦ Σαβίνου, Basil XCI 183 A; τὸν κύριόν μου τὸν τιμιώτατον καὶ εὐλαβέστατον Θεόδοτον τὸν διάκονον, Chrysostom XLIII 633. Cf. also Basil LXVIII 161 A, LXXXIX 180 C, XC 181 D, XCII 184 B, CXXXVI 228 A; Chrysostom LXI 643, LXVII 645; Atticus 349 C; Theodoret XXIV 1205 A, XXXVII 1216 A, LXX 1240 B, CXXXI 1348 D.

Other instances of the use of εὐλαβέστατος as a title for members of the clergy are as follows: for subdeacons, τὸν εὐλαβέστατον Γερόντιον τὸν ὑποδιάκονον, Theodoret X 1184 A and also Basil CCXIX 332 E; for a lector, τὸν τιμώτατον καὶ εὐλαβέστατον Ὑπάτιον τὸν ἀναγνώστην, Theodoret XI 1184 C; to monks, τοῖς εὐλαβεστάτοις καὶ θεοφιλεστάτοις πατράσι μοναχοῖς, Cyril of Alexandria XXVI 140 C and also Athanasius 26 1172 A, Gregory of Nazianzus CCXXXVIII 380 C, Cyril of Alexandria XIX 125 C.

For the clergy in general there are several examples: τῶν ὄντων εὐλαβεστάτων κληρικῶν, letter of the emperors to John of Antioch VI 1461 B; cf. also Theodoret LXXXI 1261 C, LXXXIII 1268 D, LXXXVI 1280 B, CXII 1312 A, 1312 D. In Chrysostom CXVIII 673, the title is applied to bishops and priests.

There is one instance of its being addressed to a deaconess: εἰδυῖα τοίνυν, δέσποινά μου τιμωτάτη καὶ εὐλαβεστάτη, . . . Chrysostom CIII 663.

We have found the following passages in which εὐλαβέστατος is used as a title of the emperor: οἱ εὐλαβέστατοι καὶ καλλίνικοι ἡμῶν βασιλεῖς, Paul of Emesa 165 B and also Athanasius 25 324 B. It also appears with reference to the emperor's sisters: ταῖς εὐλαβεστάταις δεσποίναις, Cyril of Alexandria LXX 341 B.

For the laity, εὐλαβέστατος is not a common title. There are but two instances for laymen: δέσποτά μου αἰδεσιμώτατε καὶ εὐλαβέστατε, Chrysostom XLVI 634 and CCXVI 730. It is more common for laywomen: ταῖς κοσμιωτάταις ἀληθῶς καὶ εὐλαβεστάταις ἀδελφαῖς Εὐσταθίᾳ καὶ Ἀμβροσίᾳ, Gregory of Nyssa III 1; cf. also Chrysostom XXXIII 629, XXXIX 631, LVII 640, XCVIII 660. The following examples are addressed to the laity as a group: καὶ τί λοιπὸν ἔτι θαυμαστὸν ὃ μέλλω γράφειν, ἀγαπητοί, εἰ τὰς κατ' ἐμοῦ ψευδεῖς διαβολὰς καὶ τοῦ εὐλαβεστάτου ἡμῶν λαοῦ ἐκθήσομαι, Alexander of Alexandria I 564 A; τῷ εὐλαβεστάτῳ καὶ πιστοτάτῳ καὶ φιλοχρίστῳ λαῷ τῆς ἐν Κωνσταντινουπόλει ἁγίας τοῦ Θεοῦ Ἐκκλησίας ἡ σύνοδος, Theodoret CLVI 1448 C.

There are a few instances of its being addressed to persons who are not identified: Basil CXIX 302 C, CXXIV 214 C, CXXXI 223 D, CCLI 387 B; Chrysostom XLIX 635, LI 636; John of Antioch V 248 B; Cyril of Alexandria LXIII 328 B, LXXVIII 361 C; Theodoret XLVII 1224 D.

θεοφιλεία: n., *divinely favored Self.*

There are few instances of the occurrence of this title in the literature examined. It is recorded by Preisigke as a title.

The examples seem to indicate that it was used for the clergy: to Atticus, bishop, τοῖς παρὰ τῆς σῆς θεοφιλείας ἐπεσταλμένοις ἐν τυχών, ἐγγεγράφθαι μὲν τὴν Ἰωάννου προσηγορίαν, ἐν ταῖς ἱεραῖς ἐμάνθανον δέλτοις, Cyril of Alexandria LXXVI 352 C; to Eunomius, priest, ἠρώτησέ με ἡ θεοφιλεία σου, τί . . . Nilus III 30, 385 B; to Casiana, deaconess, ἐπειδὴ δὲ τὴν φιλοσοφίαν οἶδα τῆς σῆς θεοφιλείας, τοὺς παραμυθητικοὺς προσενεγκεῖν ἐθάρρησα λόγους, Theodoret XVII 1196 A; to an unknown addressee, ἀλλ᾽ ἴσων δόξειεν ἂν τῇ σῇ θεοφιλείᾳ σκληρὸς εἶναί τις καὶ ἀφιλάλληλος ὁ παρ᾽ ἐμοῦ λόγος, Cyril of Alexandria LXXVIII 361 C.

CHAPTER II

SECULAR TITLES

Titles addressed specifically to the laity are most conveniently divided into four groups: those ordinarily applied to the emperor, to the emperor and other laymen, to laymen alone, and to laymen and women.

TITLES OF THE EMPEROR [1]

The emperor received the most varied and extravagant titles. The empress, since she shared his office, was honored with several of his titles.

αὔγουστος: adj. *august;* and n., *Augustus.*

Αὔγουστος as a title of the Roman Emperor is merely a transliteration of the Latin word *Augustus.* Moulton and Milligan state that in papyri it replaced the Greek title Σεβαστός at the time of the Emperor Constantine. From the evidence furnished by the letters, it came into use about the middle of the fourth century. In the works of Athanasius, we find both forms; Σεβαστός occurs only in letters which are quoted, while Αὔγουστος was used by Athanasius himself in addressing the Emperor.

The passages in which it occurs are as follows: Κωνστάντιος Νικητὴς Αὔγουστος ᾿Αθανασίῳ, Constantius to himself in Athanasius 25 624 B; θεοφιλέστατε Αὔγουστε, Athanasius 25 596 A; Αὔγουστε βασιλεῦ θεοφιλέστατε, Cyril of Jerusalem 1176 A; τὸν φιλανθρωπότατον Αὔγουστον Οὐάλεντα, Peter of Alexandria quoted in Theodoret, H. E. IV 22, 13; μοι, τὸν ᾿Ιουλιανόν, τὸν ἀρχιερέα, τὸν καίσαρα, τὸν αὔγουστον, τὸν . . . , Julian LVII. Cf. also Cyril of Jerusalem 1165 A; Athanasius 25 253 B, 341 A, 341 B, 349 C, 360 B, 385 C, 581 A, 597 A, 597 C, 600 A, 608 B, 617 B, 624 D, 625 D, 640 A, 640 B, 641 A, 641 C, and 26 692 B, 696 B, 792 A, 816 C, 817 A, 817 C.

The feminine form Αὐγούστη, *Augusta,* is found in Theodoret addressed to the empress: τῇ θεοφιλεστάτῃ καὶ εὐσεβεστάτῃ Αὐγούστῃ,

---

[1] For titles addressed rarely or not exclusively to the emperor, cf. Index under *emperor.*

CXXXIX 1364 A; cf. also XLIII 1220 C, CXXXVIII 1360 D, CXL 1364 D.

βασιλεία: n., *Royalty, Sovereignty.*

Βασιλεία is addressed only to the emperor. It appears in the letters for the first time about the middle of the fourth century, but there are two interesting passages cited from the Septuagint [2] in which βασιλεία has the concrete meaning of *King* or *His Majesty*: καὶ Γοθολία ἡ μήτηρ Ὀχοζείου εἶδεν ὅτι ἀπέθανεν ὁ υἱὸς αὐτῆς, καὶ ἀπώλεσεν πᾶν τὸ σπέρμα τῆς βασιλείας, IV Kings XI 1; καὶ εἶδον τὴν ἰσχὺν τῆς βασιλείας καὶ ὁρμήματα τῶν δυνάμεων, καὶ ἐξέκλιναν ἀπ' αὐτῶν, I Mac. VI 47.

The examples in the letters are not numerous: ἀποσταλέντα σε παρὰ τῆς βασιλείας αὐτοῦ, Athanasius 25 393 A; ἀνακτᾶταί σε τοίνυν ἡ ἡμετέρα βασιλεία, Jovian referring to himself in Athanasius 26 813 B; πρώτας ταύτας ἐξ Ἱεροσολύμων πρὸς τὴν θεοφιλῆ σου βασιλείαν ἀποστέλλω γραμμάτων ἀπαρχάς, σοί τε πρεπούσας ἀποδέξασθαι, κἀμοὶ παρασχεῖν, Cyril of Jerusalem 1165 A. Cf. also Cyril of Jerusalem 1168 A; Athanasius 26 700 B; Isidorus IV [3] 144, 1225 A; Theodoret CLII 1441 C; Julian LXXXI,[4] referring to himself.

βασίλειον: n., *Royalty, Sovereignty.*

Βασίλειον as a title occurs only in the letter of the Arian leaders to the Emperor Jovian: δεόμεθά σου τοῦ κράτους καὶ τοῦ βασιλείου σου καὶ τῆς εὐσεβείας σου, ἄκουσον ἡμῶν, Athanasius 26 820 B; δεόμεθά σου τοῦ κράτους καὶ τοῦ βασιλείου, 820 B; cf. also 821 C.

γαληνότατος: adj., *most serene;* as a substantive, *most serene Sir.*

Γαληνότατος is used only in referring to the emperor. The instances of its occurrence are very rare: ἤδεις ἡμᾶς πρὸ τῆς χθές, γαληνότατε, ἐπ' ἀπληστίᾳ χρημάτων μὴ πολιτεύεσθαι, Basil XLI 124 C; φείσασθαι ἡμῶν τοίνυν θέλησον, γαληνότατε, Basil XLI 124 D; ἀλλὰ ταῦτα πάντα λέλυκεν ὁ γαληνότατος βασιλεύς, διὰ τὴν τῆς ὑμετέρας μεγαλοπρεπείας σπουδήν, Theodoret CXXXIX 1361 D. Letter XLI

---

[2] Liddell and Scott, new edition, s. v.

[3] Critics are of the opinion that this letter was addressed to the Empress Pulcheria.

[4] This letter is considered spurious but of early date; cf. Wright, p. xlii.

of St. Basil is generally regarded as spurious, but at any rate, the letter existed in Byzantine times.[5]

γαληνότης : n., *Serenity.*

This title is given only to the emperor or empress. The few examples of its use occur in two authors of the fifth century, Cyril and Theodoret, and in letter XLI of Basil to Julian, which is considered unauthentic by most critics.[6] Moulton and Milligan cite the title as common in late papyri.

Basil uses the title as follows: ὡς γυνή τις προσέλευσιν ἐποιήσατο ἐπὶ τῆς σῆς γαληνότητος ἐπ' ἀπωλείᾳ παιδὸς αὐτῆς φαρμακευθέντος, XLI 124 E. Theodoret addresses it to the Empress Pulcheria : ἐλπίζω δὲ ὅτι ἡ ὑμετέρα γαληνότης θεραπεύσει τὰ τῆς πόλεως τραύματα καὶ ταῖς ἄλλαις δικαιοπραγίας ἐπιθήσει καὶ ταύτην, XLIII 1221 A. The remaining illustrations are in the third person : γέγονε γὰρ ἀναγκαία φροντὶς τῇ γαληνότητι αὐτοῦ τῶν Ἐκκλησιῶν ἡ ὁμοψυχία, Cyril of Alexandria XLIII 224 A, also XXXI 153 C ; πότε γὰρ ἡμεῖς τὴν αὐτοῦ γαληνότητα περὶ πράγματος ἠνωχλήσαμεν, ἢ τοὺς μεγάλους ἄρχοντας, ἢ . . . , Theodoret LXXIX 1256 D.

εὐσέβεια : n., *Worship.*

As a title εὐσέβεια is addressed regularly to the emperor. There are, however, a few examples which are addressed to the clergy. It occurs very frequently in Athanasius and Theodoret, once in Basil and Chrysostom, but there are no illustrations in Gregory of Nazianzus, Gregory of Nyssa, and Cyril of Alexandria.

The emperors used this title in referring to themselves. The following illustrations appear in the letters of the emperors to Athanasius and to John of Antioch : οὐ παρεῖδεν ἡ ἀκάματος ἡμῶν εὐσέβεια, Athanasius 25 341 B ; πρὸς τὴν ἐμὴν συνελθεῖν εὐσέβειαν βούλομαι, Athanasius 25 401 D ; παρὰ τῆς ἡμετέρας εὐσεβείας, John of Antioch VI 1461 C.

The title also occurs in the third person applied to the emperor : μετὰ τῶν παίδων τῆς εὐσεβείας αὐτοῦ, Athanasius 25 393 B ; ἀλλὰ τηρῆσαι τῇ εὐσεβείᾳ αὐτοῦ τὴν ἀκρόασιν, Athanasius 25 393 B ; cf. also

[5] Cf. Deferrari, Vol. I, p. 230.
[6] Ibid.

Athanasius 25 393 A and Theodoret LXXIX 1256 C, 1256 D. It is used with reference to the emperor and his sons, ταῦτα αὐτὰ εἰς γνῶσιν ἀνενεγκεῖν τῇ εὐσεβείᾳ αὐτῶν, Athanasius 25 385 C; also to the emperor and empress, ἀντιβολήσατε αὐτῶν τὴν εὐσέβειαν παρεῖναι τοῖς πραττομένοις, Theodoret CXXXVIII 1361 A.

The passages in which it occurs as a title of direct address to the emperor are as follows: ἐπιγνῷ παρ' αὐτῶν ἡ σὴ εὐσέβεια, Athanasius 26 792 C; τῇ σῇ εὐσεβείᾳ μετὰ σπουδῆς ἄγομεν εἰς γνῶσιν, Cyril of Jerusalem 1168 A; ἴστω ὑμῶν ἡ εὐσέβεια, Theodoret CLII 1441 C. Cf. also Athanasius 25 601 A, 601 B, 612 B, 616 C, 620 A, 620 B, 620 C, 621 B, 621 C, 624 C, 625 B, 628 A, 628 B, 628 C, 628 D, 629 A, 632 B, 637 B, 640 B, 640 C, 640 D, and 26 696 B, 792 C, 813 B, 813 C, 817 A, 820 B; Cyril of Jerusalem 1172 A; Theodoret CLII 1441 B, 1441 C, CLVII 1452 A, 1453 A, 1453 B, 1453 C, CLVIII 1453 D, 1456 A, 1456 B, 1456 C, CLXI 1460 D, 1461 B, 1461 C, 1464 A. There are two instances of its being addressed to the sisters of the emperor: μὴ τῆς ἰάσεως παρὰ τῆς ὑμετέρας εὐσεβείας ἐπιτεθείσης, Theodoret XLIII 1221 A; ἕτερα γνωρίζειν τῇ ὑμετέρᾳ προσδοκήσαντες εὐσεβείᾳ, τὰ ἐναντία δηλῶσαι ἠναγκάσθημεν, Theodoret CLIII 1441 D.

In the following passages it is addressed to members of the clergy: to bishops, ταῦτα καὶ τῇ σῇ εὐσεβείᾳ δηλῶ, Athanasius 26 1181 A, and also Alexander of Alexandria I 552 A, Basil CCLXV 409 A, Theodoret CXXXII 1349 D; to a priest, τὴν σὴν εὐσέβειαν εὐφήμως τῆς ἐμῆς μνησθῆναι σμικρότητος, Theodoret LXII 1233 B; to an archimandrite, ὥσπερ ἀμέλει καὶ νῦν τῆς σῆς εὐσεβείας τὰ γράμματα τῆς ἱερᾶς σου ψυχῆς παρέδωκε τὴν εὐσέβειαν, Theodoret L 1225 D; to monks, ἀναγκαῖον ἡγησάμην δηλῶσαι τῇ εὐσεβείᾳ ὑμῶν, Athanasius 25 692 A, and οὔτε θεασάμενος πώποτε τὴν σὴν εὐσέβειαν, Theodoret CXLIII 1368 C.

εὐσεβέστατος: adj., *most worshipful, right worshipful.*

The title εὐσεβέστατος is found in all the outstanding authors of the fourth and fifth centuries, except Basil and Synesius. It is usually addressed to the emperor, but there are occasional examples of its application to members of the clergy. Moulton and Milligan record its use in papyri from the end of the second century.

The passages in which εὐσεβέστατος is addressed to the emperor are very numerous: εὐξώμεθα περὶ τῆς σωτηρίας τοῦ εὐσεβεστάτου Αὐγούστου Κωνσταντίου, Athanasius 25 608 B; πεισθήτω δὲ διὰ σοῦ καὶ ὁ εὐσεβέστατος βασιλεύς, Gregory of Nazianzus CXXX 225 A; καὶ ταῦτα ἐτολμᾶτο παρὰ γνώμην τοῦ εὐσεβεστάτου βασίλεως, Chrysostom to Pope Innocent 533; τοῦ γράμματος τῶν εὐσεβεστάτων καὶ φιλοχρίστων βασιλέων, Cyril of Alexandria XXVIII 145 B. Cf. also Eusebius of Caesarea quoted in Theodoret H. E. I 12, 17; Athanasius 25 233 B, 264 C, 277 A, 316 B, 321 C, 324 C, 385 C, 393 A, 584 B, 597 A, 597 C, 601 C, 616 D, 640 B, and 26 692 B; Cyril of Jerusalem 1165 A; Gregory of Nazianzus CCII 333 C; Gregory of Nyssa II 13; Chrysostom 530, 531, 532; Cyril of Alexandria XVI 105 A, XXIII 133 A, XXXI 153 C, XXXVII 169 C, XXXIX 173 C, XL 184 A, 184 C, 185 A, XLIII 224 A, XLIX 253 D, LXX 341 B, LXXII 344 D, LXXVI 357 C; John of Antioch III 164 B, IV 169 D, 172 A, 172 B, VII 1448 A; Atticus 349 D; Theodoret CX 1304 D, 1305 A, CXXXIII 1352 B, CXXXVIII 1361 B, CXXXIX 1361 C, CLIII 1444 B, CLIV 1448 A, CLVI 1449 A, 1449 D, CLX 1457 C, 1457 D, CLXI 1460 A, CLXX 1477 C, 1480 D, 1481 C, 1481 D.

Εὐσεβέστατος appears as a title of the empress three times in the letters of Theodoret: τῇ εὐσεβεστάτῃ καὶ θεοφιλεστάτῃ Αὐγούστῃ, CXL 1364 D; cf. also CXXXVIII 1360 D, CXXXIX 1364 A.

There are the following examples of its application to bishops in the letters of Cyril of Alexandria: καὶ ἔγραψα μὲν τῷ εὐσεβεστάτῳ ἐπισκόπῳ τῆς Ἀντιοχέων, LXX 341 A; cf. also XI 85 A, XIII 96 A, XXXIX 176 C, LVII 320 C. It occurs also as follows: to an archimandrite, ὁ πάντα εὐσεβέστατος καὶ θεοφιλέστατος πρεσβύτερος καὶ ἀρχιμανδρίτης Μεκίμας, Theodoret CXXV 1337 D; to monks, τοῖς εὐσεβεστάτοις καὶ συνετωτάτοις συντετυχότες μονάζουσιν, Theodoret CXLI 1365 C; to the laity, καὶ τί λοιπὸν ἔτι θαυμαστὸν ὃ μέλλω γράφειν, ἀγαπητοί, εἰ τὰς κατ' ἐμοῦ ψευδεῖς διαβολὰς καὶ τοῦ εὐσεβεστάτου ἡμῶν λαοῦ ἐκθήσομαι, Alexander of Alexandria I 564 A.

The following title belongs properly here in the discussion of εὐσεβέστατος: ἐπὶ δὲ σοῦ, δέσποτα, πανευσεβέστατε βασιλεῦ, 1168 B. Cyril of Jerusalem has made the ordinary imperial title more forceful by prefixing παν-.

εὐσεβής: adj., *worshipful.*

Εὐσεβής occurs rarely as a title, but in every case, the term is addressed to the emperor: τοῦτο δὲ καὶ τῷ εὐσεβεῖ καὶ φιλοχρίστῳ ἡμῶν βασιλεῖ ἐγνωρίσαμεν, John of Antioch VII 1448 C; τοῦτο, εὐσεβεῖς βασιλεῖς, τοῦτο ὀρθοδοξίας σύστασις, Theodoret CLXI 1457 D; cf. also Isidorus IV 144, 1225 A; Cyril of Alexandria XXIII 136 D.[7]

ἡμερότης: n., *Clemency.*

Ἡμερότης is addressed to the emperor and to laymen of high station. There are no examples in Gregory of Nyssa, Chrysostom, and Cyril of Alexandria. It occurs once in Julian and Libanius.

The emperors use the term in referring to themselves. There are the following examples from letters quoted by Athanasius: εἰς τὸ στρατόπεδον τῆς ἐμῆς ἡμερότητος ἐπειχθῆτε, 25 404 B; cf. also 25 341 A, 373 B. Julian addresses it once to himself: ὅθεν αὐτῷ προαγορεύομεν ἀπιέναι τῆς πόλεως, ἐξ ἧς ἂν ἡμέρας τὰ τῆς ἡμετέρας ἡμερότητος γράμματα δέξηται παραχρῆμα, Julian XXIV.

The title appears in Athanasius and Theodoret addressed to the emperor: ἐκεῖνο μέντοι συνορᾷ μεθ' ἡμῶν καὶ ἡ σὴ ἡμερότης, Athanasius 26 792 C; τὰ . . . γράμματα τῆς ὑμετέρας ἡμερότητος, Theodoret CLVIII 1456 A; cf. also Athanasius 25 621 B, and Theodoret CLVIII 1456 C.

Basil and Gregory of Nazianzus use ἡμερότης as a title for laymen of high standing: ἐπεὶ δὲ ἱκέτευσα τὴν σὴν ἡμερότητα ὑπὲρ τοῦ ἑταίρου ἡμῶν Ἑλλαδίου τοῦ πρωτεύοντος, Basil CCLXXXI 453 E; καὶ μηδὲν ἀνάξιον μὲν αὐτοῦ, ἀνάξιον δὲ τῆς σῆς ἡμερότητος ἢ εἰπών, ἢ γράψας περὶ αὐτοῦ, Gregory of Nazianzus CCXIX 360 A. Cf. also Basil XXXIV 113 B, LXXV 171 A, LXXVI 171 D, CXLVIII 238 B, CLXXVIII 264 C; Gregory of Nazianzus CIV 204 C; Libanius, ͵ανκθ' 3.

Twice ἡμερότης occurs in letters which are without address: Basil LXXXVIII 180 A, CCCVIII 442 B.

---

[7] From its use as a title of the emperor, εὐσεβής seems to have taken the connotation of *imperial;* for example, τοῖς εὐσεβέσιν ὑμῶν . . . γράμμασι, Theodoret CLII 1440 D; τῆς εὐσεβοῦς ὑμῶν βασιλείας, Isidorus IV 144, 1225 A. This use of the term is clearly transferred from a designation of the emperor himself to the things of the emperor.

καλλίνικος: adj., *victorious.*

The title καλλίνικος is applied only to the emperor. It has a similar use in papyri.[8] The examples are as follows: ἐπὶ παρουσία τοῦ δεσπότου ἡμῶν τοῦ εὐσεβεστάτου καὶ καλλινίκου βασιλέως Κωνσταντίου Αὐγούστου, . . Athanasius *26* 692 B; οἱ εὐλαβέστατοι καὶ καλλίνικοι ἡμῶν βασιλεῖς, Paul of Emesa 165 B; ἡ τοῦ καλλινίκου βασίλεως μικρο-ψυχία, Theodoret CXII 1309 A; cf. also Theodoret CXII 1312 A, CXIX 1329 B, LXXIX 1256 C, LXXX 1257 C.

κορυφή: n., *Eminence.*

Theodoret alone makes use of the title κορυφή and always for the emperor: ὥστε τοίνυν μηδεμίαν ταραχὴν ἢ θόρυβον ἐν τῷ κοινῷ γενέσθαι συνεδρίῳ, θεσπισάτω ὑμῶν ἡ φιλόχριστος κορυφὴ δύο ἑκάστῳ μητροπολίτῃ, συνεῖναι, CLXI 1461 A; διὰ τὰ εὐσεβῆ γράμματα τῆς θεοφιλοῦς ὑμῶν κορυφῆς, CLXI 1461 C; cf. also CXIX 1329 B, CLII 1441 A, CLVIII 1456 A. Theodoret uses it once in the third person as a title of the emperor and empress: πρὸς δὲ τούτοις ἱκετεύσατε αὐτῶν τὴν θεοφιλῆ κορυφήν, CXXXVIII 1360 D.

κράτος: n., *Majesty, Mightiness.*

In the letters examined, the title κράτος is addressed exclusively to the emperor and empress. Investigations in papyri disclose the same usage.[9]

We have found examples of its use for the emperor in Athanasius, Cyril of Jerusalem, and Theodoret. They are as follows: δέομαί σου τοῦ κράτους, ἄκουσόν μου, letter of the Arian leaders quoted in Athanasius *26* 821 D; ὑπὲρ τοῦ θεοφιλοῦς σου κράτους ἐν τοῖς ἁγίοις τόποις πεποιημένοι τε καὶ ποιησόμενοι, Cyril of Jerusalem 1172 A; ἡ πρὸς τὸ ὑμέτερον κράτος ἀπολογία, Theodoret CLXI 1460 A. Cf. also the letter of the Arian leaders in Athanasius *26* 820 B, 821 B, 821 C; Theodoret CLVII 1452 A, 1452 B, 1452 D, 1453 C, CLVIII 1456 A, CLXI 1460 C, 1460 D, 1461 A, 1461 C.

Theodoret addresses it to the emperor and empress: εἰ δὲ βούλεται αὐτῶν τὸ κράτος τὴν παλαιὰν πρυτανεῦσαι ταῖς Ἐκκλησίαις εἰρήνην,

---

[8] Preisigke s. v.
[9] Preisigke s. v.

CXXXVIII 1361 A; ἀντιβολῆσαι αὐτῶν τὸ κράτος, CXL 1365 A; also to the empress alone, ἱκετεύω τὸ ὑμέτερον κράτος, XLIII 1220 C.

μέγιστος: adj., *Maximus.*

This adjective is applied to the emperor by themselves and is the equivalent of the Latin *Maximus.* A like usage occurs in papyri.[10] Examples are as follows: Νικητὴς Κωνσταντῖνος Μέγιστος Σεβαστὸς τοῖς ἐν Τύρῳ συνελθοῦσιν ἐπισκόποις, Athanasius 25 401 C; Αὐτοκράτωρ Καῖσαρ Ἰουλιανὸς Μέγιστος Σεβαστὸς Ἀλεξανδρέων τῷ δήμῳ, Julian XXI; αὐτοκράτορες, καίσαρες, νικηταί, τροπαιοῦχαι, μέγιστοι, καὶ σεβαστοί, Θεοδόσιος καὶ Οὐαλεντινιανός, Ἰωάννῃ ἐπισκόπῳ Ἀντιοχείας, John of Antioch VI 1457 C, the letter of the emperors. Cf. also the letters of the emperors quoted in Athanasius 25 348 A, 348 C, 360 B, 369 A, 373 A, 632 D, 636 B.

νικητής: n., *Conqueror.*

Νικητής is a title generally used by the emperors in referring to themselves: Κωνστάντιος νικητὴς Αὔγουστος Ἀθανασίῳ, Athanasius 25 341 A; Νικητὴς Κωνσταντῖνος Μέγιστος Σεβαστὸς τοῖς ἐν Τύρῳ συνελθοῦσιν ἐπισκόποις, Athanasius 25 401 C; αὐτοκράτορες Καίσαρες, νικηταί, τροπαιοῦχαι, μέγιστοι, καὶ σεβαστοί, Θεοδόσιος καὶ Οὐαλεντινιανός, John of Antioch VI 1457 C. Cf. also Athanasius 25 341 C, 348 A, 348 C, 349 C, 369 A, 624 B, 632 D, 636 B, 792 A; Cyril of Alexandria XXIII 136 D.

νικήφορος: adj., *victorious.*

This title is used in referring to the emperor. It is found only in Theodoret: τῷ νικηφόρῳ καὶ φιλοχρίστῳ βασιλεῖ, CXXXIX 1361 D; cf. also CXL 1364 D.

σεβαστός: n. and adj., *Augustus.*

Σεβαστός is the Greek title for the Roman emperor, corresponding to the Latin *Augustus.* According to the testimony of papyri, Σεβαστός is the older form of address which was later replaced by the transliterated form, Αὔγουστος, at the time of Constantine.[11] In the letters, however, there are several examples of its use after

---

[10] Preisigke s. v.
[11] Moulton and Milligan s. v.

the time of Constantine. The title was used most frequently by the emperors in referring to themselves.

The examples are as follows: ὁ δεσπότης ἡμῶν Κωνσταντῖνος ὁ Σεβαστός, ὁ ἐμὸς πατήρ, letter quoted in Athanasius 25 405 C; τῶν δεσποτῶν ἡμῶν σεβαστῶν, letter quoted in Athanasius 25 401 B; Αὐτοκράτωρ Καῖσαρ Ἰουλιανὸς Μέγιστος Σεβαστὸς Ἀλεξανδρέων τῷ δήμῳ, Julian XXI; Αὐτοκράτορες Καίσαρες, νικηταί, τροπαιοῦχαι, μέγιστοι καὶ σεβαστοί, Θεοδόσιος καὶ Οὐαλεντινανὸς, Ἰωάννῃ ἐπισκόπῳ Ἀντιοχείας, letter of emperors to John of Antioch VI 1460 A. Cf. also the following instances in letters quoted by Athanasius: to Constantine, 25 360 B, 369 A, 373 A, 401 C; to Constantius, 25 348 A, 348 C, 632 D, 636 B, and 26 692 B.

φιλανθρωπία: n., *Benevolence, Clemency.*

The title φιλανθρωπία is generally addressed to the emperor. This is the usage of Athanasius who employs the term most frequently. There are rare examples in the Cappadocians and these are addressed to laymen of high official rank.

The emperors used the title in referring to themselves: πειραθεὶς ἡμῶν τῆς φιλανθρωπίας, Constantine quoted in Athanasius 25 341 B; τοῖς οἰκοῦσι δὲ τὴν Ἔδεσσαν προαγορεύομεν ἀπέχεσθαι πάσης στάσεως καὶ φιλονεικίας, ἵνα μή, τὴν ἡμετέραν φιλανθρωπίαν κινήσαντες, καθ᾽ ὑμῶν αὐτῶν ὑπὲρ τῆς τῶν κοινῶν ἀταξίας δίκην τίσητε, ξίφει καὶ φυγῇ καὶ πυρὶ ζημιωθέντες, Julian XL.

Athanasius addresses it to the emperors in the following passages: ἰδοὺ γὰρ ἡ μὲν σὴ φιλανθρωπία, 25 637 C; τὰ γράμματα τῆς σῆς φιλανθρωπίας ἐδεξάμεθα, 26 792 B; cf. also 25 316 B, 597 A, 608 A, 616 D, 624 A, 624 D, 628 D, 629 A, 632 B, 632 C, 637 B, 641 A, 641 C, and 26 792 C. The term occurs once as a title in the third person, referring to the emperors: ὅπως ἡ φιλανθρωπία αὐτῶν καὶ τοὺς ἔτι κάμνοντας καὶ πιεζόμενος ἀνεθῆναι κελεύσῃ, 25 321 C.

The passages in which the title is given to laymen of high standing are few: οὗ μάλιστα πάντων μέλειν τῇ ἀξιαγάστῳ σου φιλανθρωπίᾳ πεπείσμεθα, Basil CX 203 C; ταῦτα μὲν ποιείτω καὶ λεγέτω πρὸς τὴν σὴν φιλανθρωπίαν ἡ τοῦ πλάσματος πόλις, Gregory of Nazianzus CXLI 241 A and also CV 205 B; ἡ σὴ φιλανθρωπία νικήσειε, Gregory of Nyssa VII 4.

φιλάνθρωπος: adj., *benevolent, clement*.

Athanasius uses the positive of the more usual title, φιλαν-θρωπότατος, in addressing the emperor: ὁ φιλάνθρωπος βασιλεύς, 25 592 A; cf. also 25 252 C and 253 A.

φιλανθρωπότατος: adj., *most benevolent, most clement*.

As a title, φιλανθρωπότατος is addressed to the emperor. The examples are rare: συγχώρησον εἰπόντι μοι ταῦτα, φιλανθρωπότατε Αὔγουστε, Athanasius 25 600 A; τὸν φιλανθρωπότατον Αὔγουστον Οὐάλεντα, Peter II of Alexandria quoted in Theodoret H. E. IV 22, 13; ὁ φιλανθρωπότατος ἡμῶν βασιλεύς, Synesius LXXIX 1444 C.

It appears to be used as a title addressed to priests by Theodoret in letter CXXXII 1349 B: εἰς ἐκείνους δὲ μόνον ἀφορᾶν ἀξιῶ, καὶ τῶν φιλανθρωποτάτων ἱερέων τοὺς μὲν ἢ δικηκότας θρηνεῖν, τοὺς δὲ παρορῶντας ἐλεεῖν, καὶ τὸν μὲν τῆς Ἐκκλησίας ὀδύρεσθαι κλύδωνα.

φιλόχριστος: adj., *Christian, Christ-loving;* as a substantive, *Christian Sir*.

The adjective φιλόχριστος is generally a title of the emperor, but it is used occasionally to refer to laymen of distinction and, in rare instances, to ecclesiastics. It appears in Athanasius, Nilus, Cyril of Alexandria, and Theodoret.

The passages in which it is addressed to the emperor are as follows: τῷ φιλοχρίστῳ καὶ εὐσεβεστάτῳ βασιλεῖ, Cyril of Alexandria XVI 105 A; ἐκ θεσπίσματος τῶν εὐσεβεστάτων καὶ φιλοχρίστων βασιλέων, John of Antioch III 164 B; κατὰ τὰ εὐσεβῆ τῶν φιλοχρίστων ἡμῶν βασιλέων θεσπίσματα, Theodoret CLIII 1444 D. Cf. also Athanasius 25 612 C, 629 D; John of Antioch III 164 D, IV 172 A, V 248 B, VII 1448 A, 1448 C; Cyril of Alexandria XXIII 133 A, XXVIII 145 B, XXXI 153 C, XL 184 A, 185 A, LXX 341 B, LXXII 344 D; Theodoret CXXXVIII 1360 A, 1360 D, CXXXIX 1361 C, 1361 D, CXL 1364 D, CLII 1441 A, 1441 C, CLIII 1444 A, 1444 B, CLIV 1445 B, 1448 A, CLVI 1449 A, 1449 D, CLVIII 1456 A, CLX 1457 C, 1457 D, CLXI 1461 A, CLXX 1481 C. Φιλόχριστος has the force of a title in the following passage which refers to the emperor Constans, οὐ γὰρ οὕτως ἦν εὐχερὴς ὁ φιλόχριστος ἐκεῖνος, οὐδὲ τηλικοῦτος ἤμην ἐγώ, ἵνα περὶ τοιούτων ἐκοινολογούμεθα, Athanasius 25 600 A.

Theodoret uses φιλόχριστος as a title of the empress: τὴν φιλό-χριστον Αὐγούσταν, CXXXVIII 1361 B.

There are the following examples of φιλόχριστος for the laity: to the Senate of Constantinople, τῇ θεοφιλεῖ καὶ φιλοχρίστῳ συγκλήτῳ ἡ ἁγία σύνοδος ἐν Κυρίῳ χαίρειν, Theodoret CLIV 1445 A; to the people of Constantinople, τὴν διδασκαλικὴν ἀρδείαν προσφέροντα τοῖς φιλοχρίστοις λαοῖς, Theodoret CII 1296 C and also LXXXIII 1269 A, CLVI 1448 C; to laymen of distinction, ὦ φιλόχριστοι, Theodoret LXXXVIII 1284 A, and also XLVII 1225 A, XCIV 1288 C, XCVII 1292 A.

Examples addressed to ecclesiastics are rare: to a bishop, Εὐτρόπιον τὸν φιλόχριστον, Athanasius 25 648 B; to deacons, τοὺς γὰρ φοβουμένους τὸν Κύριον δοξάζεις, φιλόχριστε, Nilus II 277, 340 B and II 144, 265 D.

TITLES FOR LAYMEN [12]

The titles addressed to laymen fall into three divisions: titles given to laymen of official rank, to laymen of high standing, and to men of letters.

TITLES FOR LAYMEN OF OFFICIAL RANK.

There are several titles which are reserved for laymen who were officials of the government. There does not seem to be any specific title connected with each of the various civil offices.

δίκη: n., *Justice.*

Gregory of Nazianzus alone uses δίκη as a title. He addresses it three times to government officials: to Olympius, prefect of Arianzus, τὴν ἀθλίαν Φιλουμένην δι' ἐμαυτοῦ προσάγω σοι, καὶ τῇ σῇ δίκῃ προσπεσουμένην, καὶ ὑμῖν τὰ δάκρυα στήσουσαν, οἷς συντρίβει τὴν ἡμετέραν ψυχήν, CIV 204 C; αὐτὸς μὲν οὖν δηλαδὴ πράξεις, ὁ παρίσταται τῇ σῇ δίκῃ καὶ τῷ κατευθύνοντί σε πρὸς πάντα Θεῷ, CXLIV 245 C; to Gregory, archon, εἰ μή σοί τε παρασταίη καὶ τῇ σῇ δίκῃ στῆναι πρὸς τὸν πονηρὸν δαίμονα, CXCV 320 A.

---

[12] For titles addressed rarely or not exclusively to laymen, cf. Index under *laymen.*

ἐξουσία: n., *Authority.*

'Εξουσία is addressed only to laymen of high civil authority. We find examples of its use in Basil, Gregory of Nazianzus, and Theodoret. It occurs also in papyri.[13]

The passages in which the title occurs are as follows: οἱ δὲ νῦν ἀπογραψάμενοι, ὡς οὐ λαβόντες παρὰ τῆς ὑπερφυοῦς σου ἐξουσίας πρόσταγμα, ἀπεγράψαντο, πλὴν εἰ μή πού τινες ἄλλως εἶχον ὑπὸ τῆς ἡλικίας τὴν ἄφεσιν, Basil CIV 199 A; καὶ δῶς αὐτῷ θάρσος ὥστε φωνὴν ῥῆξαι ἐπὶ τῆς μεγάλης σου καὶ ὑπερφυοῦς ἐξουσίας, Basil CCLXXIX 423 A; κάλλιστον εὗρον παραθέσθαι αὐτὸν τῇ σῇ ἐξουσίᾳ, Gregory of Nazianzus CXXXVII 233 A. Cf. also Basil CCXXV 344 D; Gregory of Nazianzus CXXVI 221 A, CXLI 241 A; Theodoret XCIV 1288 C.

ἡμερώτατος: adj., *most clement.*

We have found only two examples of the title ἡμερώτατος, both addressed to men of high civil authority: to Anthemius, prefect of the East, τὸν δέσποτά μου τὸν ἡμερώτατον 'Ανθέμιον, Chrysostom CXLVII 699; to Pentadius, civil governor of Egypt, μετὰ τὸν ἡμερώτατον καὶ φιλοσοφώτατον Πεντάδιον, Synesius CXXVII 1508 A.

καλοκἀγαθία: n., *Excellency.*

The title καλοκἀγαθία is generally addressed to laymen of high official rank. It is used most frequently by Basil and Gregory of Nazianzus. Preisigke records it as a title.

The passages in which it is addressed to laymen are as follows: ἀεὶ μαθόντας ὅτι οὐκ ἄχρηστος αὐτοῖς ἡ παρ' ἡμῶν πρεσβεία πρὸς τὴν ἀνυπέρβλητόν σου καλοκἀγαθίαν γεγένηται, Basil XV 95 A; ἃ δ' ἂν παρὼν ἐδεήθην τῆς σῆς καλοκἀγαθίας, ταῦτα καὶ ἀπὼν ἐθάρρησα, Gregory of Nazianzus CXXVI 221 A. Cf. also Basil XV 94 E, XXXII 111 D, LXXXIV 176 E, CXII 204 B; Gregory of Nazianzus XXI 56 C, CIII 204 B, CXXXVI 232 C, CLXX 280 B, CLXXXI 296 B, CXCV 320 A, CXCIX 328 A, CCVIII 345 A.

The title is given to the emperor by Athanasius: ἐφ' οἷς ἔπραξαν παρὰ γνώμην τῆς σῆς καλοκἀγαθιάς, 25 637 C. It also occurs in Basil XLI 124 C, a letter which is considered spurious: to Julian, ἐντεθύμημαι γὰρ καθ' ἑαυτὸν ὡς ἐγώ τε αὐτὸς καὶ ἡ σὴ καλοκἀγαθία κοινῶς μεμαθήκαμεν τὰ ἱερὰ καὶ βέλτιστα γράμματα.

[13] Moulton and Milligan s. v.; Preisigke s. v.

It occurs for laymen of the scholarly class: οὐ βάρβαρον τὸ ἐπίταγμα τῆς ἀμιμήτου σου καλοκἀγαθίας, ἀλλ' Ἑλληνικόν, μᾶλλον δὲ Χριστιανικόν, Gregory of Nazianzus LXII 124 A; ὡς ἐδέξατο τῆς σῆς καλοκἀγαθίας τὰ γράμματα ἐκεῖνος, ὃν οὐ βούλομαι λέγειν, Isidorus V 199, 1452 B.

There are two instances where the identification of the person addressed is uncertain: Basil CCLXXIII 419 E, CCCXXV 449 D. In the latter case the title is addressed to a certain Magninianus, called Count Magninianus in some editions.

λαμπρότατος : adj., *most splendid, most brilliant.*

The title λαμπρότατος is always given to laymen of very high official rank. We find examples of its use in Athanasius, Synesius, Isidorus, and Theodoret. It is very common in papyri.[14]

The passages in which it occurs are as follows: ὑπατείᾳ Ἰουλίου Κωνσταντίου τοῦ λαμπροτάτου πατρικίου, ἀδελφοῦ τοῦ εὐσεβεστάτου βασιλέως Κωνσταντίνου τοῦ Αὐγούστου, καὶ Ῥουφίνου Ἀλβίνου, τῶν λαμπροτάτων, Θὼθ δεκάτῃ, Athanasius 25 385 C; μισθὸς ἀρετῆς ἔπαινος, ὃν εἰσφέρομεν Μαρκελλίνῳ τῷ λαμπροτάτῳ, Synesius LXII 1405 C. Cf. also Athanasius 25 385 A, 385 C, 389 C, 392 C, and 26 692 B; Julian LXXX; Nilus I 319, 197 B; Theodoret XXIII 1204 C.

The title occurs in the superscription of several letters of Isidorus to persons who are not known; for example, Χρύσῃ λαμπροτάτῳ, II 78, 520 B; Δωροθέῳ λαμπροτάτῳ, III 175, 865 B; cf. also III 252, 932 A; III 361, 1016 C; III 392, 1032 C; III 394, 1033 A; IV 43, 1093 C; V 250, 1481 D.

λαμπρότης : n., *Splendor, Brilliancy.*

Like the adjective λαμπρότατος, this title is used only in addressing laymen of official rank. We find examples of its occurrence in Athanasius, Chrysostom, Nilus, and Theodoret. The title appears in papyri.[15]

The passages in which it occurs are as follows: τούτου ἕνεκεν ἀνενεγκεῖν ἐπὶ τὴν σὴν λαμπρότητα ἠπείχθημεν καὶ ἐπιδοῦναι τόδε τὸ μαρτύριον, Athanasius 25 392 B; παρακαλοῦμέν σου τὴν λαμπρότητα,

---

[14] Moulton and Milligan s. v.; Preisigke s. v.
[15] Moulton and Milligan s. v.

Chrysostom CXXXIX 695; ἅρπάσει γὰρ δῆλον ὅτι προθύμως ἡ σὴ
λαμπρότης τὴν θεόσδοτον δωρεάν, Theodoret LXXVII 1245 A. Cf.
also Nilus III 302, 349 B; Chrysostom CXXXIX 695, CCXXXVI
740; Theodoret XXXVII 1213 D, 1216 A.

μεγαλόνοια: n., *Magnanimity*.

The title μεγαλόνοια is generally addressed to laymen of high
official rank. Examples of its use are found in Basil, Gregory of
Nazianzus, Isidorus, and Theodoret. Preisigke also records it.

The passages in which μεγαλόνοια is addressed to laymen of high
station are as follows: καταλέγειν μὲν πάντας τοὺς δι᾽ ἡμᾶς εὐεργετηθέντας
παρὰ τῆς σῆς μεγαλονοίας, οὐ ῥᾴδιον; Basil CLXXVII 163 E; διὰ τοῦτο
συγγινωσκέτω μὲν ἡμῖν ἡ σὴ μεγαλόνοια, Gregory of Nazianzus CXXX
225 A; πυθόμενος ὑπὸ τῆς πόλεως πάσης τὴν σὴν παρακεκλῆσθαι μεγαλόνοιαν, ἄτοπον ᾠήθην ἀμοιρῆσαι τῆς τοιαύτης, Isidorus II 25, 473 B.
Cf. also Basil LXXVI 171 C, LXXXIV 177 A, LXXXVI 178 E,
CIV 198 D, CXXXVII 228 E, CCXXV 344 D, 345 B, CCLXXXI
423 E, CCCXIII 444 C; Gregory of Nazianzus XXI 56 C, XXII
57 A, CXXIX 224 B, CXLI 244 A, CXXXI 228 A.

Twice it appears for a scholasticus: εἰ τοίνυν καὶ τῇ σῇ μεγαλονοίᾳ,
εὐμερία ἐλπίδος κρείττων ἐπέστη, μηδὲν ἀπηχές, μηδὲ λέγε, μηδὲ πρᾶττε,
Isidorus III 283, 960 A; θερμότερον περὶ τὴν σὴν διετέθημεν μεγαλόνοιαν,
Theodoret XLVI 1224 C.

Basil uses μεγαλόνοια twice in referring to a bishop: ἀνάγκη δὲ καὶ
τὰ λειπόμενα παρὰ τῆς σῆς μεγαλονοίας ὁρισθῆναι, LX 155 B; cf. also
CCXLI 370 E.

In the following instances, the addressee is uncertain or unknown: Basil LXXIV 169 B, CCLXXIII 419 E, CCCXXVII
450 D; Isidorus II 78, 520 B.

μέγεθος: n., *Greatness*.

The title μέγεθος is addressed to laymen of high rank and official
position. It occurs frequently in Theodoret, but only once in Basil,
Firmus, and Procopius. It is common in papyri.[16]

The examples are as follows: τούτου χάριν πάντες ἤλθομεν ἐπὶ τὸ
ἱκετεῦσαι τὸ μέγεθός σου, μηδὲν ἀγανακτῆσαι τῇ ἀναβολῇ τῆς ἀπαντήσεως,

---

[16] Moulton and Milligan s. v.; Preisigke s. v.

Basil CCXXV 345 A; ὁ λαμπρότατος Διονύσιος πρὸς τὸ ὑμέτερον μέγεθος
ἔδραμεν, Theodoret XXIII 1204 C; ἐγὼ μὲν οὖν αὐτὸν πρὸς τὸ ὑμέτερον
ἐξενάγησα μέγεθος, Theodoret XXXIV 1212 C.   Cf. also Theodoret
XL 1216 D, XLII 1217 B, XLIV 1221 B, 1221 C, XLV 1221 D,
1224 A, LVIII 1229 C, LXXI 1241 A, LXXIV 1244 B, LXXIX
1256 A, LXXIX 1256 C, 1257 A, LXXX 1257 B, 1257 C, 1260 A,
LXXXI 1261 A, LXXXIX 1284 A, XCII 1288 A, XCIV 1288 C,
XCV 1289 B, XCVI 1292 A, XCVII 1292 B, CXI 1308 C, CXIX
1328 C, 1329 C, CXXXVIII 1361 A, CXXXIX 1361 D, 1364 A,
CXL 1364 B, 1364 D.

The following examples are uncertain, but they are probably
also addressed to laymen of rank: Firmus XXX 1501 C; Theodoret
LIX 1232 A, CXX 1332 A, CLX 1457 D; Procopius LXX 2773 D.

περίβλεπτος: adj., *admired.*

As a title, περίβλεπτος is addressed only to laymen of high official
rank. The examples are infrequent and occur only in Theodoret
and two minor writers. It is common in late papyri as a term
of address.[17]

The examples are as follows: τῷ κυρίῳ μου τῷ θαυμασιωτάτῳ καὶ
περιβλέπτῳ Ἀριστολάῳ τῷ τριβούνῳ καὶ νοταρίῳ, John of Antioch V
248 C; γράμμα ἐξέπεμψαν διὰ τοῦ περιβλέπτου τριβούνου καὶ νοταρίου
Ἀριστολάου, Paul of Emesa 165 B; τὸν περίβλεπτον Φίλιππον τὸν τῆς
ἡμετέρας πρωτεύοντα πόλεως, Theodoret XLVII 1224 D.   Cf. also
John of Antioch IV 172 A; Theodoret XLII 1217 C, XLIV 1221 C,
XLVII 1225 A.

πρᾳότης: n., *Clemency.*

Πρᾳότης occurs as a title in the following passages: to Arcadius,
imperial treasurer, ἀποπέμψασθαι μετὰ πάντων καὶ αὐτοὺς, ἀνυμνοῦντας
τὴν σὴν πρᾳότητα, Basil XV 95 A; to Modestus, prefect, ὁ πάλαι
ἐπόθεις ἀκοῦσαι, νῦν ἥκει σοι θαυμαστή τις ἀφορμὴ πρὸς τὴν τῆς καταδίκης
λύσιν, ἢ κατ' οὐδὲν μὲν δίκαιον ἐπέπεσεν Ἀνυσίῳ τῷ καλῷ, τὸ μὴ παγῆναι
δὲ βεβαίως ὑπὸ τῆς σῆς ἔπαθε πρᾳότητος, Libanius σ' 1.

The emperors used the title in referring to themselves as follows:
καὶ τὰς ὑπὲρ τῆς ἡμετέρας πρᾳότητος προθύμως εὐχὰς ἀναπέμπετε εἰς Θεόν,
Athanasius 26 813 B; cf. also 25 348 B, 349 A.

[17] Moulton and Milligan s. v.   Cf. also Preisigke.

TITLES FOR LAYMEN OF HIGH STANDING

The following titles are addressed to men of distinction for wealth, nobility of descent, and social influence, as well as for recognition of official rank.

ἄριστος: adj., *my excellent;* as a substantive, *excellent Sir, very good Sir,* and in less formal address, *my very good friend.*

As a title, ἄριστε is generally addressed to laymen of high station and to friends with whom the writer's relations are rather formal. It occurs in the letters of the fourth and fifth centuries but we find no examples in those of Athanasius, John Chrysostom, and Cyril of Alexandria. There are several illustrations of its use in Libanius, who frequently uses the adjectival form, ἄριστος, as a title, but we find no examples of this usage among Christian writers.

The occurrence of ἄριστε as a title for laymen of consequence is as follows: ἀλλὰ τί οὐκ ἐπιφοιτᾷς ἡμῖν, ὦ ἄριστε, ὥστε παρόντας ἡμᾶς ἀλλήλοις περὶ τῶν τοιούτων διαλεχθῆναι, Basil IX 91 C; μὴ μεταβαλλέτω σε, ὦ ἄριστε, ὡς ἕνα τῶν πολλῶν εὐμερίας αὖρα, Isidorus III 225, 933 B; σὸν μὲν ἔργον, ὦ ἄριστε, τὸ καὶ τοὺς ἄλλους εἰς τὴν τῶν ἐγκαινίων πανήγυριν καλεῖν, Theodoret LXVII 1237 A. Cf. also Basil LVI 150 D, LXXIV 168 C, LXXXIV 177 B, XCIV 188 D, CCX 314 B, CCXVI 324 B; Gregory of Nazianzus XI 41 C; Isidorus I 86, 241 C; II 136, 580 A; III 392, 1032 C; Theodoret LXXVI 1245 A.

The few examples of its being addressed to members of the clergy are as follows: to bishops, μὴ θαύμαζε, ὦ ἄριστε, Isidorus III 360, 1016 A and also II 127, 565 A, II 211, 652 A, V 435, 1581 A; to a monk, καὶ ξένον οὐδὲν ὑπομένεις, ἄριστε, Nilus II 52, 224 A.

Ἄριστε appears in letters addressed to unknown persons, but in each case, the person is probably a layman except in Gregory of Nyssa XVI, 4, where the addressee may be a priest. The references are: Basil CCCXLI 456 E, a letter which is probably spurious; Gregory of Nazianzus XXXI 68 C; Isidorus I 270, 341 D; Procopius LXX 2776 A.

There are also instances in which ἄριστε seems to be used partly as a title and partly in its literal sense; for example, φήσει, ὅτι, ὦ ῥητόρων ἄριστε, θαυμάζω πῶς εἰς τοὐναντίον, Isidorus II 146, 600 C.

The examples in Libanius are as follows: as a substantive, χεῖρα ὄρεξον, ὦ ἄριστε letter νθ' 2, and also νςζ' 3, χνα' 2, ψν' 3, ψξγ' 7, ‚ατξη' 3, ‚ατπ' 3, ‚αυκη' 3; as an adjective, οἶδα δὲ καὶ τὸν ἄριστον Μόδεστον, letter σβ' 2; πρὸς τὸν ἄριστον Θεόδοτον, letter ρπζ' 2; letter ‚ανβ'. 3, ‚αξζ' 3, et passim.

There is a special use of ἄριστος in the adjectival expression, ὁ πάντα ἄριστος, as a title of esteem to be translated *the most excellent*. The earliest illustration occurs in the letter of Alexander of Jerusalem to Origen: δι' ὧν σὲ ἐγνώρισα τὸν κατὰ πάντα ἄριστον καὶ κύριόν μου καὶ ἀδελφόν, quoted in Eusebius VI 14, 9. The later examples are as follows: ἀλλ' ἐκεῖνα τὰ μυθικὰ τέως καὶ ἄπιστα, πάνυ ἡμᾶς πιθανὰ νομίζειν ἐδίδαξεν ἡ περὶ τὸν πάντα ἄριστον Μάξιμον περιπέτεια, Basil CXLVII 237 C; οὐ γὰρ ἀπέθανεν ὁ πάντα ἄριστος ἐκεῖνος ἀνὴρ . . . ἀλλὰ καθεύδει, Theodoret LXIX 1237 C. Cf. also Basil CCLXXI 417 B and CCCXXXVIII 454 D, a letter which is probably spurious.

ἐνδοξότατος: adj., *most distinguished*.

'Ενδοξότατος is given as a title of esteem to eminent laymen, As such, it is found first in letters of the fifth century. Preisigke notes its use in papyri.

The passages in which it occurs are as follows: ὁ μεγαλοπρεπέστατος καὶ ἐνδοξότατος κόμης 'Ιωάννης, Cyril of Alexandria XXVII 141 C; ἐβεβαίωσε δὲ ὁ ἐνδοξότατος καὶ φιλόχριστος κύριος Φλωρέντιος, Theodoret XLVII 1225 A; τοῦ ἐνδοξοτάτου καὶ φιλοχρίστου κυρίου τοῦ Πατρικίου, Theodoret XCVII 1292 A. Cf. also Chrysostom CCXXV 735; Cyril of Alexandria XXVIII 145 A; John of Antioch VII 1448 C; Theodoret XXXIII 1212 A, LXXXII 1264 B, CX 1305 A, CLIV 1445 B.

It is addressed once to the emperor: μετὰ τοῦ ἐνδοξοτάτου Κωνσταντίνου, Athanasius *26* 696 C.

θαυμασιότης: n., *admirable Self, Excellency*.

The title θαυμασιότης is used to address laymen of distinction by Chrysostom, Theodoret, and Firmus. Preisigke records its use in papyri.

The passages in which it occurs are as follows: παρακαλῶ σου τὴν θαυμασιότητα, δέσποτε μεγαλοπρεπέστατε, Chrysostom CXCVII 721;

καὶ τούτων χάρις τοῖς ἐπὶ τῇ θαυμασιότητί σου ταῦτα πράττειν καταβαλ-
λομένοις τὴν ψῆφον, Firmus I 1481 A; ταῦτά σου τὴν θαυμασιότητα καὶ
λογίσασθαι παρακαλῶ, Theodoret XVIII 1197 A. Cf. also Chrysostom XX 623, XLI 632, XLII 633, L 636, LXXIX 651, CXXIV
678, CXXVII 688, CXLVII 699, CXCVII 722, CCI 723, CCXX
732, CCXXXIV 739, CCXXXVI 742; Firmus XX 1497 A,
XXXIX 1508 C; Theodoret XXXIII 1212 B, XXXVII 1216 A,
CXXIV 1336 B, CXXV 1337 D.

Theodoret addresses it to laywomen: ταῦτα τὴν σὴν εἰδυῖαν θαυμασιότητα, τὴν ἀνθρωπείαν φύσιν καταμαθεῖν ἀξιῶ, XIV 1188 C; cf. also
VIII 1181 C, LXIX 1237 B, 1237 C.

The following examples are addressed to persons who are unidentified, but who are probably laymen: Chrysostom LXXIII 648,
CXXXIV 692, CLXXXIX 718; Firmus XXV 1500 B.

θαυμασιώτατος: adj., *most admirable*; as a substantive, *most admirable Sir* or *most admirable friend*.

As a title, θαυμασιώτατος occurs in all the important authors of
the fourth and fifth centuries except Gregory of Nyssa and Nilus.
It is generally applied to laymen of high rank, but we have noted
three examples which are addressed to ecclesiastics. It is frequent
as a title in late papyri.[18]

The passages in which θαυμασιώτατος is used as a title for laymen
of distinction are as follows: εὐθὺς ἐπιτυχὼν ἀφορμῆς, ἐπέστειλα τῷ
θαυμασιωτάτῳ ἀνδρὶ Τερεντίῳ τῷ κόμητι, Basil CCXV 323 B; δέσποτά μου
θαυμασιώτατε, Chrysostom XCV 659; ἵνα δὲ καὶ διδάξῃς, θαυμασιώτατε,
τοὺς ἀγνοοῦντας ὅπως φρονοῦμεν, Theodoret XXI 1201 B. Cf. also
Basil LXXVII 172 B, XCIX 194 D, CIX 202 D, CX 203 B,
CCCXIII 444 B; Gregory of Nazianzus CXXXI 225 C, CXLV
248 B; Chrysostom XLII 633, LVIII 641, CXXVIII 688,
CXXXII 691, CXLIII 697, CLXXXVII 717, CXCIV 720,
CXCVII 722, CCI 723, CCIV 724, CCXXXVI 740; John of
Antioch IV 172 A, V 248 C; Cyril of Alexandria XXXVII 169 B,
XL 184 C, XLVIII 249 B, 252 C; Theodoret XXIX 1208 B, XXX
1208 C, XXXI 1209 A, XXXII 1209 D, XXXIV 1212 C, XXXV
1212 D, XXXVI 1213 B, CLX 1457 C.

---

[18] Moulton and Milligan s. v. Cf. also Preisigke.

It is addressed to ecclesiastics as follows: to a bishop, Εὐφρατίωνα τὸν θαυμασιώτατον, Athanasius 25 648 B; cf. also Basil CCXIV 321 B, Amphilochius 93 C; to a priest, ἴσθι, ὦ θαυμασιώτατε, Isidorus III 349, 1005 A.

In the following instances, the addressees are not identified, but most of them, from the context of the letters, appear to be laymen: Synesius CXXIX 1509 D; Chrysostom XX 623, L 636, LI 637, LXXIII 648, CXXXIV 692, CLXXV 712, CLXXXVIII 717; Theodoret LIX 1232 A.

μεγαλοπρέπεια: n., *Magnificence.*

The title μεγαλοπρέπεια is addressed to laymen of high rank. It is found in John Chrysostom, Firmus, and very frequently in Theodoret. Thus it seems to have been first used by writers of the fifth century. It appears in papyri.[19]

The examples are as follows: συνδεδέσθαι μετὰ ἀκριβείας τῇ μεγαλοπρεπείᾳ τῇ σῇ, Chrysostom CXCIV 720; προσδοκῶ τὴν μεγαλοπρέπειάν σου, Firmus IV 1484 C; τὴν δὲ ὑμετέραν μεγαλοπρέπειαν παρακαλῶ, Theodoret LXXXI 1264 A. Cf. Chrysostom XLI 632, XLII 633, LXXIX 650, CXXIV 678, CXXXII 691, CXLVII 699, CXCVII 721; Firmus XII 1489 C, XX 1497 C, XXVI 1500 C, XXIX 1501 B; Theodoret XV 1192 B, XXII 1204 B, XXXIII 1212 A, 1212 B, XXXIV 1212 C, XXXVII 1213 D, 1216 A, XLII 1217 B, 1220 B, XLIV 1221 B, XLV 1221 D, 1224 B, XLVI 1224 C, LVII 1229 C, LXV 1236 B, LXXII 1241 C, 1241 D, LXXVI 1244 D, LXXIX 1256 A, LXXX 1257 B, XCI 1285 B, XCII 1288 A, XCIII 1288 A, XCVI 1289 C, 1289 D, XCVII 1292 A, XCVIII 1292 C, XCIX 1292 D, 1293 A, CIII 1296 D, CXIV 1324 A, CXIX 1329 B, 1329 C, CXXXIX 1361 D, CXL 1364 B, CLIV 1445 A, CLIX 1457 A.

The following examples are uncertain: Chrysostom LI 636, CLXXXIX 718; Firmus XXI 1497 B, XXVIII 1501 A; Theodoret V 1180 C, XXIX 1208 B, XLI 1217 B, LV 1229 B, LIX 1232 A, LXXIV 1244 A, XC 1284 D, 1285 A, CV 1324 B, CXX 1329 D, CLX 1457 C.

---

[19] Moulton and Milligan s. v.; Preisigke s. v.

μεγαλοπρεπέστατος: adj., *most magnificent.*

This title is addressed to laymen of high station. It is found in the letters of John Chrysostom, Cyril of Alexandria, and Theodoret, and thus appears to have come into use in the early part of the fifth century. It is recorded as occurring in papyri.

The examples are as follows: δέσποτα θαυμασιώτατε καὶ μεγαλοπρεπέστατε, Chrysostom CXXXII 691; παρὰ τοῦ μεγαλοπρεπεστάτου κόμητος Κανδιδιανοῦ, Cyril of Alexandria XXIII 136 D; ἐπὶ τοῦ μεγαλοπρεπεστάτου ὑπάρχου τοῦ κυρίου Φλωρεντίου, Theodoret XLIV 1221 B. Cf. also Chrysostom CXCVII 721, CCI 723; Firmus XXXIX 1508 C; John of Antioch I 1450 A, VII 1448 C; Cyril of Alexandria XXIII 136 A, XXVII 141 C, 141 D, 144 A, XXIX 145 A, XXXVII 168 C, 169 B, XLIV 228 C; Theodoret XXIX 1208 B, XXX 1208 C, XXXI 1209 A, XXXII 1209 D, XXXIII 1212 A, XXXIV 1212 C, XXXV 1212 D, XXXVI 1213 B, LXX 1240 A, LXXIX 1256 A, LXXXII 1264 B, CX 1305 A, CLII 1441 A, CLIII 1444 A, 1444 B, CLIV 1445 B, CLVIII 1456 B.

The following examples are addressed to persons whose rank is not known: Synesius XXI 1360 B, Chrysostom XLII 633, Theodoret VII 1180 D.

μεγαλοφυΐα: n., *Magnanimity.*

The title μεγαλοφυΐα is generally addressed to laymen of high standing. We find examples only in Basil and Theodoret.

Basil uses it twice in addressing bishops: πάλιν οὖν καὶ ἐνταῦθα τῇ σῇ μεγαλοφυΐᾳ πρέπειν τὴν τῶν τηλικούτων διακονίαν ἐλπίζομεν, ὥστε . . . , LXVI 160 B; μετὰ μὲν γὰρ τῆς σῆς μεγαλοφυΐας καὶ πρὸς τοὺς μεγάλους ἀποδύσασθαι πειρασμοὺς οὐκ ὀκνοῦμεν, XCVIII 192 A.

The remaining examples, addressed to laymen of distinction, are as follows: ὥστε, εἰ, μήπω τῆς κατ᾽ ὀφθαλμοὺς ἡμῖν συντυχίας τὴν γνῶσιν σου τῆς μεγαλοφυΐας χαρισαμένης, φαμὲν εἶναι φίλοι σου καὶ συνήθεις, Basil LXIII 156 D; τοῦτο δὲ μόνον τὴν ὑμετέραν μεγαλοφυΐαν ἀντιβολῶ, Theodoret XLII 1217 D; ταῦτα δὲ ἐξαιτῶ παρὰ τῆς ὑμετέρας μεγαλοφυΐας, Theodoret CXXXVIII 1361 A. Cf. also Basil LXXVI 171 B, LXXXVI 179 B, XCIX 195 D, CIV 199 B, CX 203 B, CXI 203 D, CCLXXIV 420 A, CCLXXIX 422 E, CCLXXXI 423 D, CCCVI 441 C; Theodoret XXIII 1204 C, XLII

1220 B, XLIV 1221 C, XLV 1224 A, LVII 1229 C, LXV 1236 C, LXXI 1241 A, LXXIX 1256 A, 1256 B, 1256 D, 1257 A, LXXXI 1260 B, 1264 A, LXXXVIII 1281 D, LXXXIX 1284 C, XCII 1285 C, XCIII 1288 B, XCIV 1288 C, 1288 D, XCV 1289 A, XCVI 1289 C, CXI 1308 A, 1309 A, CXXI 1332 C, CXXXVIII 1360 D, CXXXIX 1316 C.

Titles for Men of Letters

There is a distinct group of titles which belong to men of the class including rhetors, sophists, and advocates. They are listed below.

ἐλλογιμώτατος: adj., *most notable*; as a substantive, *most notable Sir*.

'Ελλογιμώτατος is used as a title by Isidorus and Theodoret, generally for scholars. Preisigke notes its use as a title of honor.

It occurs as follows: ἀποδοτέον, ὦ ἐλλογιμώτατε, Isidorus IV 16, 1064 C; τὸν ἐλλογιμώτατον 'Αθανάσιον τὸν ῥήτορα, Theodoret XIX 1197 B. Cf. also Isidorus V 317, 1520 C; Theodoret XX 1197 C, XXII 1204 A.

Isidorus makes use of it three times in addressing men of other occupations: to a bishop, III 10, 734 B; to a priest, III 163, 857 B; to a corrector, III 263, 944 B.

λογιότης: n., *Eloquence*.

The title λογιότης is found in the Cappadocians, in Nilus, Synesius, and Isidorus. It appears to be addressed to laymen of the scholarly class. The title occurs in papyri.[20]

Gregory of Nazianzus addresses it three times to laymen of official rank, but it is quite possible that they were literary men as well: καὶ τοῦτο φθεγξόμεθα πρὸς τὴν σὴν λογιότητα, CXCVIII 325 A; cf. also CXCV 317 C, CXCIX 325 B.

The certain examples of its being addressed to laymen of the scholarly class are as follows: οὐδὲ τότε ἠγνόουν, ὅτε ἐπέστελλον τῇ λογιότητί σου, ὅτι πᾶσα θεολογικὴ φωνή, ἐλάττων μέν ἐστι τῆς διανοίας τοῦ λέγοντος, Basil VII 80 Λ; ἐπεὶ οὖν ἤδη μετὰ τὸν κόρον πρὸς ὕπνον

---

[20] Moulton and Milligan s. v.; Preisigke s. v.

κατεφερόμην, παραστησάμενος τὸν ὑπογράφοντα, ταύτην σου τῇ λογιότητι καθάπερ ἐνύπνιον τὴν ἐπιστολὴν ἀπελήρησα, Gregory of Nyssa XX 21; ἀλλ' εἰδότα ὡς ἀρκεῖ γράμμα τῆς σῆς λογιότητος, Firmus II 1484 A. Cf. also Basil I 70 C, CL 239 E, 240 D, CCLXXI 417 C, CCCXXXVII ²¹ 454 B; Gregory of Nazianzus XXXVIII 80 B, CLXXV 288 A, CCXXXIV 377 A; Gregory of Nyssa XI 1; Nilus III 153, 453 D; Isidorus V 125, 1396 D; Firmus VI 1488 A.

The following examples are addressed to persons quite unknown: Basil LXXVII 172 A, CCXII 318 C, CCCX 443 A; Gregory of Nazianzus CXLVIII 253 B; Synesius CXXXII 1520 A; Firmus XXVII 1500 D, XXXI 1504 A, XXXIII 1504 C, 1505 A.

παίδευσις: n., *Culture.*

The title παίδευσις is used in addressing men of the scholarly class. It is noted as a title in papyri.²²

The passages in which it occurs are as follows: μηνύσαντος ἀθρόως μοί τινος περὶ τῶν γραμμάτων τῆς μονογενοῦς σου παιδεύσεως, Gregory of Nyssa XIII 2; μάλα ἀκριβῶς οἶδε σου ἡ παίδευσις, Isidorus V 349, 1537 D; . . . ἵνα τὴν σὴν διδάξωσιν ἃ πεπόνθασαι παίδευσιν, Theodoret X 1184 B. Cf. also Basil CCCXLIV 457 D, a letter which is probably spurious; Gregory of Nyssa XI 2; Isidorus V 115, 1392 D; V 185, 1437 B; V 192, 1448 B; V 198, 1452 A; Theodoret CXXIV 1336 B.

TITLES FOR LAYMEN AND LAYWOMEN

The titles listed below are addressed to laymen and laywomen.

εὐγένεια: n., *Nobility.*

Εὐγένεια is usually addressed to persons of rank, both men and women. Its use is rather general. It is very common in John Chrysostom, but it does not occur in Athanasius nor in Isodorus. It is also found in papyri.²³

For laymen of rank, it occurs as follows: ὥστε εἰ καὶ μὴ μέμνημαι δεξάμενος γράμματα τῆς εὐγενείας σου, πείθομαι ἐπεσταλκέναι σε ἡμῖν, Basil

---

²¹ This letter is probably spurious.
²² Preisigke s. v.
²³ Moulton and Milligan s. v.; Preisigke s. v.

LVI 150 B; προσάγω τῇ σῇ εὐγενείᾳ, Gregory of Nazianzus CCVII 344 A; καὶ ἤδη ἐπεστάλκαμέν σου τῇ εὐγενείᾳ, δέσποτά μου τιμώτατε καὶ εὐλαβέστατε, Chrysostom CCXVI 730. Cf. also Basil LXXIII 166 D, LXXXIII 176 A, CL 239 B, CLV 244 A, CCXCII 431 B; Gregory of Nazianzus XXIX 64 C, LXIII 125 B; Gregory of Nyssa XX 14; Chrysostom LXI 642, LXXXIII 652, XCV 659, C 661, CXXVIII 688, CLXXI 710, CLXXXVII 717, CXCVIII 722, CCV 726.

Εὐγένεια is addressed to women in the following passages: πάνυ ἠθύμησα τοῖς γράμμασιν ἐντυχὼν τῆς εὐγενείας σου, ὅτι σε πάλιν αἱ αὐταὶ περιέχουσιν ἀνάγκαι, Basil CVII 200 E; ἀλλ᾽ οὐχὶ τὴν σὴν εὐγένειαν ὑπεμνήσαμεν, Gregory of Nazianzus LXXIX 149 B; γράφοντες πρὸς τὴν εὐγένειαν τὴν σήν, Chrysostom LVII 640. Cf. also Basil CLXXIV 261 E, 262 A, CCLXXXIII 424 D, CCXCVII 434 C; Chrysostom XLIII 633, LII 637, LVII 640, CLXVIII 709, CLXXIX 713, CXCII 719, CCXXVII 736, CCXXIX 737, CCXXXII 738, 739.

We have found only four instances of its application to the clergy; to bishops, ἀποστεῖλαι δὲ ἐν χάρτῃ γεγραμμένον ἐκώλυσάν με οἱ μετ᾽ ἐμοῦ ἀδελφοί, εἰπόντες παρὰ τῆς εὐγενείας σου ἐντολὰς ἔχειν ἐν σωματίῳ γράψαι, Basil CCXXXI 354 E, and also Gregory of Nyssa XXI 3; to priests, ὁμολογοῦντες τῇ εὐγενείᾳ τῇ σῇ, Chrysostom CLXXIII 711, and also CLXXIII 710. The title εὐγένεια was probably given to these clergymen out of consideration for their social rank rather than as a title connected with their ecclesiastical office.

There are several passages in which εὐγένεια is addressed to persons who are unidentified but whom we may judge to be laymen from the context of the letters: Basil XI 92 D, XXXVI 114 B, CI 196 E, CCLXXVIII 422 C, CCCXV 445 A; Chrysostom XX 623, XXIV 626, XXXI 628, XLVIII 635, L 636, LI 636, CXXI 675, 676, CXXXIV 692, CLXXII 710, CLXXV 711, 712, CXCVI 721, CCIX 728; Theodoret XIII 1185 D.

εὐγενέστατος: adj., *most noble.*

The title εὐγενέστατος is used in addressing laymen and laywomen of rank. It occurs most frequently in the letters of St. John Chrysostom, but rarely in those of St. Basil and Theodoret. No other author makes use of it. We have found but one instance of its application to an ecclesiastic, that is, to the lector Theodotus, who was also of noble rank, Chrysostom CXXXVI 694. Preisigke records its use in papyri.

In the following passages εὐγενέστατος is addressed to laymen of high rank: ταῦτ' οὖν εἰδότες, κύριοί μου τιμιώτατοι καὶ εὐγενέστατοι, Chrysostom LXV 644; δέσποτά μου αἰδεσιμώτατε καὶ εὐγενέστατε, Chrysostom CXLI 696; cf. also Chrysostom C 661.

As a title for laywomen, we have found the following illustrations: τὴν εὐγενεστάτην θυγατέρα ἀσπαζόμεθα διὰ σοῦ, Basil CCXCVI 434 B; ταῦτ' οὖν εἰδυῖα κυρία μου κοσμιωτάτη καὶ εὐγενεστάτη, Chrysostom XVIII 623; τραγῳδίας ἄξιον τὸ κατὰ τὴν εὐγενεστάτην Μαρίαν διήγημα, Theodoret LXX 1240 A. Cf. also Chrysostom XLIII 633, XCIX 661, CLXVIII 709; Theodoret LXX 1240 B.

Basil uses it once in addressing the children of a philosopher: τὰ δὲ εὐγενέστατα παιδία, XVII 96 A.

In the following instances, the title is given to persons who are unidentified but who seem to be laymen: Chrysostom XXXV 630, XLIV 634, XLVIII 635, CXCVIII 722.

CHAPTER III

ECCLESIASTICAL AND SECULAR TITLES

Certain titles were not confined to either clergy or laity, but were addressed to persons of both classes. This group of titles has four subdivisions according to the following specific uses: titles for the emperor and bishops; titles for bishops and laymen; titles for bishops, laymen, and laywomen; general titles for persons of all classes.

TITLES OF THE EMPEROR AND BISHOPS

Titles used in address either to the emperor or to bishops are these:

θεοφιλέστατος: adj., *most divinely favored*; as a substantive, *most divinely favored Sir*.

The title θεοφιλέστατος is addressed very frequently to bishops. It is also common as a title of the emperors, and there are a few instances of its application to the lower clergy. It is found in all the important authors of the fourth and fifth centuries, except Gregory of Nyssa and Nilus. Preisigke records its use in non-literary sources.

The instances of its being addressed to the emperor are as follows: ἐπὶ παρουσίᾳ τοῦ θεοφιλεστάτου ἡμῶν βασίλεως, Eusebius of Caesarea quoted in Theodoret H. E. I 12, 2; πίστευε, θεοφιλέστατε βασιλεῦ, Athanasius 25 604 A; δέδοται μὲν οὖν τῇ ἁγίᾳ συνόδῳ προθεσμία ἡ ἁγία Πεντηκοστὴ παρὰ τῶν θεοφιλεστάτων βασιλέων, Cyril of Alexandria XXIII 133 C. Cf. also Eusebius of Caesarea in Theodoret H. E. I 12, (7, 14, 17); Athanasius 25 248 B, 253 C, 308 D, 316 B, 321 C, 341 A, 352 C, 373 A, 392 B, 393 A, 397 C, 397 D, 400 A, 596 A, 613 C, 617 B, 624 D, 625 D, 640 A, 641 A, and 26 717 C, 717 D, 792 B, 792 C, 816 C, 817 A, 820 A; Cyril of Jerusalem 1165 A, 1168 B, 1172 B, 1173 A, 1176 A; Chrysostom 532; Cyril of Alexandria XXXIX 173 C, XLIII 224 A, XLVIII 252 A; Theodoret CLIV 1445 B, CLX 1457 B. Theodoret addresses it to the em-

press: τῇ θεοφιλεστάτῃ καὶ εὐσεβεστάτῃ Αὐγούστῃ, CXXXIX 1361 D;
cf. also CXXXVIII 1360 D, CXL 1364 D.

Θεοφιλέστατος is applied very frequently to bishops. The examples are as follows: ὁ θεοφιλέστατος ἐπίσκοπος ὁ ἀδελφὸς ἡμῶν Βοσπόριος, Basil LII 144 D; τῶν σὺν αὐτῷ θεοφιλεστάτων ἐπισκόπων, Cyril of Alexandria II 41 A; ὁ θεοφιλέστατος ἐπίσκοπος τῆς Περρηνῶν Ἐκκλησίας Ἀθανάσιος, Proclus XIII 881 B; ἐρρωμένος ἐν Κυρίῳ ὑπερεύχου ἡμῶν, θεοφιλέστατε ἀδελφέ, Gennadius 1617 C. Cf. also Athanasius 26 813 A; Basil LXVII 160 C, LXXXII 175 D, XCII 183 C, XCV 189 B, XCVIII 192 B, 192 E, XCIX 194 C, CXX 211 C, CXXVII 218 B, 218 C, CXXVIII 219 D, CL 240 D, CLXIII 254 A, CLXXXI 265 C, CXCV 287 A, CC 298 C, CCXV 323 C, CCXVII 325 A, CCXIX 332 E, CCXXIII 339 D, CCXXVII 350 A, CCXLIII 372 D, CCLXIV 407 D, CCXXVII 351 B, CCXXVIII 351 C, CCXXIX 352 C, CCXXX 353 B, CCXXXI 354 C, CCXXXII 355 A, CCLXVI 413 A; Gregory of Nazianzus XIX 53 A, CLXXII 297 A, CLXXXIII 300 A, CLXXXIII 300 C, 301 A, CLXXXIV 301 B, CLXXXV 304 A, 304 B; Synesius CV 1488 B; Chrysostom 529, CXIV 671, CXII 669, CCXXX 737; Cyril of Alexandria II 40 C, 41 A, IV 44 C, IX 61 D, XI 80 B, 85 A, XIII 96 A, 96 C, XVII 105 C, XXIII 133 C, 136 C, XXXI 149 D, 156 D, XXXIX 176 A, 176 C, XL 185 A, 200 D, XLVIII 252 A, 252 D, XLIX 253 D, LV 316 C, LVI 320 B, LXIX 340 A, LXXVI 357 B, LXXIX 365 A; Nestorius 44 A, 49 B, 57 B; Acacius 100 B; Alypius 145 C; Maximianus 148 D, 149 B, 149 C; Paul of Emesa 165 C; Atticus 349 D; John of Antioch I 1450 A, 1452 B, 1452 C, 1452 D, 1456 D, 1457 A, II 132 B, 132 C, III 164 B, IV 169 D, 172 A, 172 B, 173 B, V 248 A, 248 B, VI 1460 B; Firmus XXXVIII 1508 A; Proclus XIII 881 A, 881 B, 881 D, 884 A, 884 C; Theodoret XIV 1189 D, XXXV 1212 D, XLIII 1220 D, LI 1228 A, LII 1228 C, LIII 1228 D, LXXX 1257 B, LXXXI 1260 D, LXXXIII 1268 B, 1268 D, LXXXIV 1276 C, LXXXV 1276 D, 1277 A, 1277 B, LXXXVI 1277 C, 1280 A, 1280 B, XCIII 1288 A, XCIV 1288 C, XCV 1289 A, XCVI 1292 A, C 1293 C, CI 1293 D, CIII 1296 D, CIV 1297 A, CV 1300 C, CVI 1300 D, CIX 1304 C, CX 1305 B, 1305 C, CXI 1308 A, 1308 B, 1308 C, CXII 1309 A, 1312 B, 1312 D, CXIII 1316 A, CXIX 1329 B, CXXI 1332 A, CXXIII 1336 A,

CXXVI 1340 A, CXXX 1344 A, 1348 C, CXXXII 1349 B, CLIII 1444 A, 1444 B, CLIV 1445 B, CLXX 1476 A, 1476 B, 1480 D; Gennadius 1617 C.

Θεοφιλέστατος is used as a title for other ecclesiastics as follows: archdeacon of Rome, CXVIII 1328 B; chorepiscopi, Theodoret CXIII 1317 C, CXVI 1325 B, CXVII 1325 C; to archimandrites, Cyril of Alexandria LXIX 337 D and Theodoret L 1225 D, CXXV 1337 D; to priests, Gregory of Nazianzus XLI [1] 85 B, CCXI 348 C, and Theodoret XIX 1197 B, XX 1197 C, LXI 1232 D, LXII 1233 C, CVIII 1301 B; to monks, Athanasius 26 1173 A, Serapion 932 A, Cyril of Alexandria XIX 125 C, Theodoret XCVII 1292 A; to a deaconess, Chrysostom I 549, 555, III 573, V 597, VIII 608, IX 608, XI 609; to the Church of Armenia, Proclus II 856 B; to the famous teacher Hypatia, Synesius IV 1341 B.

Basil addresses the title twice to Gregory of Nazianzus as follows: ὁ θεοφιλέστατος ἀδελφὸς ἡμῶν Γρηγόριος ὁ ἐπίσκοπος, XXXII 111 B; ἐπεὶ οὖν τὸν θεοφιλέστατον ἀδελφὸν ἡμῶν Γρηγόριον τὸν ἐπίσκοπον κατέλαβε πράγματα, XXXIII 112 D.[2]

In the following instances, the title is addressed to persons whose station in life is not known to us: Cyril of Alexandria LXXVIII 361 C; Theodoret CXXX 1348 B. They are probably bishops, however.

θεοφιλής: adj., *divinely favored.*

As a title, θεοφιλής occurs rarely but its usage appears to agree with that of the superlative θεοφιλέστατος. Preisigke records its occurrence also.

The title is given to the emperor: πρέπουσα θεοφιλεῖ βασιλεῖ φιλομαθὴς προαίρεσις καὶ πόθος τῶν οὐρανίων, Athanasius 26 813 B; διαφερόντως δὲ ἐπὶ τῆς σῆς ἐπιδημίας ταύτην τὴν χάριν ὡμολογήσαμεν τῷ Θεῷ καὶ τῷ θεοφιλεῖ βασιλεῖ, Basil CCXXV 344 C. And it is found

---

[1] Letter XLI is ascribed to the father of St. Gregory.

[2] The passages give rise to some interesting observations. Both letters are believed to have been written before St. Gregory's elevation to the episcopate and while he was still a monk. Accordingly, the word ἐπίσκοπος is believed to be a gloss. But Basil uses θεοφιλέστατος only with bishops in every other instance of its occurrence. It would appear then that St. Gregory was already a bishop and that ἐπίσκοπος is not a gloss.

also for bishops: ὁ μὲν θεοφιλὴς Ἑρμογένης, Isidorus V 378, 1553 B; τοῖς δυτικοῖς θεοφιλέσιν ἐπισκόποις, Cyril of Alexandria XV 100 D.

Theodoret addresses it once to the Senate of Constantinople: τῇ θεοφιλεῖ καὶ φιλοχρίστῳ συγκλήτῳ, ἡ ἁγία σύνοδος ἐν Κυρίῳ χαίρειν, CLIV 1445 A.

TITLES FOR BISHOPS AND LAYMEN

The titles which were used in addressing both bishops and laymen are as follows:

αἰδεσιμώτατος: adj., *right reverend, very reverend, most respected.*

Αἰδεσιμώτατος is a title of esteem used principally of bishops and laymen of high standing. There are a few illustrations of its use in addressing the clergy. The title is found mostly in letters of the fourth century. It occurs most frequently in Basil, but it appears also in Gregory of Nazianzus, Gregory of Nyssa, John Chrysostom, and in some letters addressed to Athanasius. There are examples in the letters of Julian.

The earliest instance of its occurrence is in the letter of Origen to Gregory Thaumaturgus: χαῖρε ἐν Θεῷ, Κύριέ μου σπουδαιότατε καὶ αἰδεσιμώτατε υἱὲ Γρηγόριε παρὰ Ὠριγένους, 88 A.

In the following passages, αἰδεσιμώτατος is applied to bishops: Ἀθανασίῳ τῷ αἰδεσιμωτάτῳ ἐπισκόπῳ, quoted in Athanasius 25 373 B; οὐδὲ ἐκείνην ἀληθῶς αὐτὸς ὁ ἐπίσκοπος διεπέμψατο, ὡς ὁ αἰδεσιμώτατος ἀδελφὸς Ἄνθιμος ἡμῖν ἀπήγγειλε, Basil LVIII 152 B; τὸν αἰδεσιμώτατον Εὐλάλιον, τὸν θεοφιλέστατον ἐπίσκοπον, Gregory of Nazianzus CLXXXII 297 A. Cf. also Athanasius 25 348 B, 361 C, 380 B, 380 C, 385 A; Basil LVIII 152 A, 152 D, LXXXIX 180 D, XCV 189 C, XCVIII 192 C, XCIX 193 B, 193 C, 194 E, CLXXVII 264 A, CCLVIII 394 A, CCCLXI [3] 463 B, CCCLXIII [3] 465 C; Gregory of Nazianzus CLXXXV 304 A; Gregory of Nyssa I 4; Chrysostom 529, CXIV 671.

The title is applied to laymen as follows: ἦλθε δέ μοι εἰς ἔννοιαν καὶ ἡ τῶν κεκληκότων ἀφοσίωσις, ὅτι παροδικὴν πρὸς ἡμᾶς ποιησάμενοι τὴν κλῆσιν διὰ τοῦ αἰδεσιμωτάτου ἀδελφοῦ Ἑλληνίου τοῦ ἐξισοῦντος Ναζιανζόν,

---

[3] Letters CCCLXI and CCCLXIII are considered unauthentic.

Basil XCVIII 191 E; ὁ αἰδεσιμώτατος υἱὸς ἡμῶν Θεοδόσιος ἧκει πρὸς τὴν σὴν λογιότητα, Gregory of Nazianzus CXCIX 325 B; ποίησον τοίνυν παρακληθῆναι τὸν δεσπότην μου τὸν αἰδεσιμώτατον Θεόφιλον τὸν κόμητα, Chrysostom IV 591. Cf. also Basil XXXV 114 A, LX 155 C, LXXI 164 D, CXXXII 225 A, CXLVIII 237 E, CXCVIII 289 C; Gregory of Nazianzus XXI 56 C, XXXIX 80 C, LXV [4] 128 B, CXLIV 215 B, CXXVII 221 B; Chrysostom XLVI 634, CXLI 696.

There are some varied examples of the general use of αἰδεσιμώτατος in addressing members of the clergy: for priests, πρὸς τὸν αἰδεσιμώτατον ἀδελφὸν καὶ συμπρεσβύτερον ἡμῶν Σακερδῶτα, Gregory of Nazianzus CCXVI 353 A, and also Basil LXIX 162 A, CCLXXI 417 D; to deaconesses, δέσποινά μου αἰδεσιμωτάτη καὶ θεοφιλεστάτη, Chrysostom I 555 and also 549. The examples of its use in the letters of Julian fall into this class: Θεοδώρᾳ τῇ αἰδεσιμωτάτῃ, the superscription of letter XXXIII to a priestess; τὸν ἀδελφὸν Ἰουλον τὸν αἰδεσιμώτατον πατριάρχην, in letter LI [5] to Hillel II, the Jewish patriarch at Alexandria.

In many cases the persons to whom the titles are addressed are unidentifiable, but most of them appear to be bishops or laymen of high station: Basil XXXI 110 E, LXIII 157 A, LXIV 157 C, LXXVIII 172 C, LXXIX 173 A, CXIX 210 C, CXX 212 B, CCLXXIII 419 D, CCLXXIV 420 A, CCLXXV 420 C; Gregory of Nazianzus CLIX 265 C; Gregory of Nyssa XXVIII 4; Chrysostom XX 623, L 636, CXCVIII 722.

ἀρετή: n., *Excellency.*

Ἀρετή is used very rarely as a title of courtesy in the letters studied, but it is cited as occurring frequently in late papyri.[6]

The examples are as follows: to Barses, bishop of Edessa, ἀλλὰ μίμνησαι τὴν σεαυτοῦ ἐν πᾶσι τελειότητα, ἵνα καὶ ἡμεῖς ἀπολαύσωμέν σου τῆς ἀρετῆς, Basil CCLXVII 414 B; to Saturninus, imperial

---

[4] Letter LXV of St. Gregory is found in the Basilian corpus as letter CLXVI.

[5] This letter is considered a forgery; cf. Wright, Introduction, p. xxii.

[6] Moulton and Milligan s. v.; Liddell and Scott, new edition s. v.; Preisigke s. v.

general, Εὐδόξιον, ἄνδρα καὶ βίῳ καὶ λόγῳ τῆς σῆς ἀρετῆς ἄξιον, Gregory of Nazianzus CLXXXI 296 B; to Palladius, magister officiorum, οὐκ ἄλλον τινὰ πρὸ τῆς σῆς ἀρετῆς, οἶδ᾽ ὅτι θήσομαι, Gregory of Nazianzus CIII 201 C.

δεσπότης: n., *Lord*.

The title δεσπότης was given most frequently to bishops. It was also addressed to the emperor and to laymen of high standing. It is a term of very great respect and usually implies that the writer is addressing a person who has authority over him. The word δεσπότης itself connotes a relationship of slave to master, while κύριος has a wider application and frequently expresses the relationship existing between the head and the members of a family.[7] Δεσπότης is one of the more common titles and examples are found in all the important authors except Gregory of Nazianzus and Gregory of Nyssa.

The passages in which δεσπότης is addressed to the emperor are as follows: τῶν δεσποτῶν ἡμῶν Κωνσταντίνου τοῦ Αὐγούστου, καὶ τῶν ἐπιφανεστάτων Καισάρων παίδων αὐτοῦ, Athanasius 25 385 C; δέσποτα, πανευσεβέστατε βασιλεῦ, Cyril of Jerusalem 1168 B. Cf. also Athanasius 25 341 B, 401 B, and 26 692 B; Cyril of Jerusalem 1172 B; Cyril of Alexandria LX 341 B.

John Chrysostom uses δεσπότης commonly in addressing laymen of rank; for example, δέσποτά μου τιμιώτατε, XXXVIII 631; ἐπειδή σε φιλῶ, δέσποτά μου αἰδεσιμώτατε καὶ εὐλαβέστατε, XLVI 634; cf. also IV 591, XIII 610, LVIII 641, LXIV 644, LXXV 649, XCV 659, CXXVIII 688, CXXXII 691, CXLI 696, CXLIII 697, CXLVII 699, CLXXXVII 717, CXCIV 720, CXCVII 721, 722, CCI 723, CCIV 724, CCIX 728, CCXVI 730, CCXXXVI 740. It occurs also in the following authors: Athanasius 25 393 B, Basil CXII 205 D, Synesius XCVII 1465 D.

There are numerous instances of its being addressed to bishops: οὐ γὰρ ἀγνοεῖς, δέσποτά μου τιμιώτατε καὶ εὐλαβέστατε, Chrysostom XXV 626; τῷ δεσπότῃ μου τῷ θεοφιλεστάτῳ καὶ ἁγιωτάτῳ συλλειτουργῷ Κυρίλλῳ, Ἰωάννης ἐν Κυρίῳ χαίρειν, John of Antioch II 132 B; εὔξασθαι δὲ ὑπὲρ ἡμῶν, δέσποτα, καταξίωσον, Theodoret CXLVI 1412 D. Cf.

[7] Thayer s. v.; Liddell and Scott s. v.

also letters quoted in Athanasius 25 568 A; Basil, the three un-authentic letters, CCCLXI 463 B, CCCLXIII 465 C, CCCLXIV 466 D; Chrysostom 529, 536, X 608, XXV 626, XXVI 626, XXVII 626, 631, XXX 628, LXXXVII 654, LXXXVIII 654, CIX 667, CXII 669, CXIV 671, CXXXI 690, CXLII 696, 701, CLX 705, CLXII 706, CLXXXIV 716, CCIV 725, CCXXX 737; Cyril of Alexandria XLIX 253 B; Acacius 100 B; Paul of Emesa 165 B; John of Antioch I 1450 A, 1452 D, 1457 A, II 132 B, 132 C, IV 169 D, 173 B, V 248 A; Theodoret XVI 1192 C, 1196 A, XXIV 1205 A, XXXV 1212 D, XXXVI 1213 C, LX 1232 B, LXXXIII 1268 B, 1273 C, LXXXVI 1280 D, CIV 1300 B, CIX 1304 C, CX 1304 D, CXII 1309 C, 1312 C, CXVI 1325 B, CXXIII 1336 A, CXXXII 1349 C, CXXXV 1353 C, CXLIII 1369 A, CLXX 1481 B. In all but very few cases, the bishop addressed is of higher rank than the writer of the letter.

Priests are given the title δεσπότης in very rare instances. This is the usage of John Chrysostom except in letter CCXL of his corpus which belongs to Constantius, priest. The passages are as follows: ἐγὼ μὲν σφόδρα ἐπιθυμῶ σὺν ἡμῖν εἶναι τὸν δεσπότην μου τὸν τιμιώτατον πρεσβύτερον, LXXVI 649; δέσποτά μου τιμιώτατε καὶ εὐ-λαβέστατε, CCXXI 733; cf. also LXXVIII 650, CI 661, CXIV 671, CCXXI 733, CCXXX 737, CCXL 746. Theodoret addresses it once to Renatus, papal representative at the Council of Ephesus: δέσποτα, CXVI 1324 C.

Chrysostom gives the title to Theodotus, who was a deacon and also of noble rank, doubtless out of consideration for his secular position rather than for his ecclesiastical office: δέσποτά μου τιμιώτατε, Chrysostom CXXXV 693.

In the following passages, the persons are unidentified: Basil CCCLXIV 465 E, 466 D, a letter which is considered unauthentic; Synesius XCVII 1465 C; Chrysostom XX 623, XXXI 628, XLI 633, XLVIII 635, L 636, LI 637, LXXIII 648, CXXI 675, CXXXIV 692, CLXXV 712, CLXXVII 712, CLXXXVIII 717, CXCVIII 722.

ὀρθότης: n., *Rectitude.*

The title ὀρθότης is used rarely. It is found for bishops or laymen of high station. Only two authors make use of it, Basil and Gregory of Nazianzus.

It is addressed to bishops as follows: μή τις τῶν αἱρετικῶν κακούργως τοῖς ἑαυτοῦ συγγράμμασι τὸ ἐμὸν ὄνομα παραγράψας, ἐλύπησέ σου τὴν ὀρθότητα, Basil XXV 104 D; cf. also Basil XC 181 B.

It occurs for laymen of rank in the following passages: ὥστε τῶν ἐν σοὶ καλῶν ἀπολαύειν, καὶ τὰ κατὰ τὸν οἶκον τὸν ἐμαυτοῦ πράγματα διὰ τῆς σῆς ὀρθότητος εὐπρεπῶς διαθέσθαι, Basil CXXXVII 228 D; αἰσχύνομαι γὰρ κατηγορεῖν ἐπὶ τῆς σῆς ὀρθότητος, οὗ πρώην ὑπερεμάχουν, Gregory of Nazianzus CXLVI 249 B; cf. also Basil CLXXVII 264 A, CCXIV 321 B, CCCX 443 B.

σύνεσις: n., *Intelligence.*

The title is generally addressed to bishops and laymen of distinction. Examples of its use occur in all authors of importance except Synesius, Cyril of Alexandria, Nilus, and Theodoret.

It is addressed to bishops as follows: τοῖς παρὰ τῆς σῆς συνέσεως ἐντυχὼν γράμμασι, Athanasius 25 369 A; τίς οὖν ταῦτα διαπράξασθαι τῆς σῆς συνέσεως δυνατώτερος, Basil LXVI 159 B; οἶδε πάντας ἡ σὴ σύνεσις, Isidorus V 79, 1373 A. Cf. also Athanasius 25 369 C, 372 A, 624 B; Basil CXIX 211 B, CLXV 256 A, CXC 282 A, 282 E, CCV 308 C, CCXVIII 331 B, CCXXXVI 360 E, CCL 385 B, CCLVIII 393 C, CCLX 399 D; Gregory of Nyssa XXIX 1 and 3; Isidorus IV 146, 1232 A; Acacius 101 A.

The title is given to laymen of distinction in the following passages: ἐπιστέλλω τῇ τελείᾳ συνέσει σου, Basil CCLXXXIV 425 A; ἃ δὲ βοηθήσεις καὶ δι' ὧν, καὶ ὅπως, τά τε πράγματα ὑποθήσεται, καὶ ἡ σὴ διασκέψεται σύνεσις, Gregory of Nazianzus XXIX 65 B. Cf. also Basil XXXIII 112 E, CCCVI 441 C; Gregory of Nazianzus XXXVIII 80 B, CC 328 B; Isidorus V 185, 1436 A.

The title occurs rarely for lower clergy: for priests, . . . οὐδεὶς ἀνήγγειλε τῇ συνέσει ὑμῶν, Basil CCXV 323 C and also Isidorus III 197, 881 B; to a deacon, ἐπειδὴ γέγραφέ σου ἡ σύνεσις, ὅτι . . . Isidorus V 197, 1449 B; to the clergy in general, . . . ἐπιστεῖλαι ὑμῶν τῇ συνέσει, Basil CCVII 309 E.

It is addressed to persons who are unknown to us: Basil CCXIII 320 D; Gregory of Nazianzus CCXI 348 C, CCXXVII 369 C; Chrysostom CXXXIV 692.

τελειότης: n., *Perfection.*

The title τελειότης is addressed most frequently to bishops, although we find several examples in Basil addressed to laymen of distinction. The title also occurs in Gregory of Nazianzus, Gregory of Nyssa, Cyril of Alexandria, and Theodoret. We note no instances of its use in John Chrysostom and in Athanasius.

It is addressed to bishops as follows: ᾔδεν ὅτι ξενίσει τὴν ἀκοὴν τῆς τελειότητός σου, Basil CXXIX 220 B; προσαγορεύομεν τὴν σὴν τελειότητα, Gregory of Nazianzus LXVI 129 C; ἀπέστειλά σου τῇ κατὰ Θεὸν τελειότητι, Theodoret CIX 1304 B. Cf. also Basil XXX 110 A, L 143 A, LVII 151 D, LXVI 159 A, LXVIII 161 B, LXIX 162 A, LXXX 173 B, 173 C, CXXIX 221 B, CLXVII 257 C, CLXXII 260 B, 260 C, CCV 308 B, CCXVII 325 A; Gregory of Nyssa XXV 2; Gregory of Nazianzus LXIV 125 C, CXXXIX 236 B, CLVII 265 A, CLXXXIV 301 C, CCII 333 C; Cyril of Alexandria XIV 97 A, XXXI 149 D, 153 D, XL 184 A, 200 A, 200 B, XLII 221 C, XLIII 224 A, 224 B, XLV 229 A, 237 C, XLVI 244 B, XLVIII 253 A, 253 B; Theodoret LXXXIII 1268 B, 1269 A, 1273 A.

In the following instances, τελειότης is addressed to laymen: ἐπεὶ δὲ ἀπελείφθης διὰ γραμμάτων αὐτοὺς ἀναγκαῖόν ἐστι προσαχθῆναί σου τῇ τελειότητι, Basil CXLII 235 B; ἄλλοι τῆς σῆς τελειότητος ἀπολαύουσιν, Gregory of Nazianzus XCIII 168 A; cf. also Basil XXVI 105 D, XXXII 112 B, XCVI 190 A, 190 D, CXII 204 B, 205 D, CCXIV 321 C, CCLXXII 418 D.

The title also occurs in the following passages: to a priest, Basil CXXXIV 225 E; to monks, Basil XXIII 102 A; to a deaconess, Theodoret CI 1296 A; to persons who are unidentified, Basil CXIV 207 D, CCXIII 320 D and Gregory of Nazianzus CCIV 340 A, CCXXIV 368 C.

φρόνησις: n., *Prudence.*

The title φρόνησις is generally addressed to bishops. There are occasional examples for laymen of distinction. Basil uses it most frequently, but it occurs also in Athanasius, Isidorus, and the pagan Julian.

The title is addressed to bishops· as follows: εὐχερῶς ἡ ὑμετέρα φρόνησις δυνήσεται κρίνειν, addressed to Athanasius in 25 624 B; λέλυται πᾶσα Ἐκκλησία, ὡς οὐδὲ ἡ σὴ φρόνησις ἀγνοεῖ, Basil LXXXII 175 B; cf. also Basil LIX 154 D, LXVI 159 A, LXVII 160 E, LXVIII 161 C, LXXXIX 180 E, CXXVIII 219 C, CXLI 234 A, CCXXXVII 366 A, CCLXIII 407 C, and Gregory of Nazianzus CCII 333 B.

Basil gives the title to laymen of distinction: γνώριζε τοίνυν τὸν ἀδελφὸν τόνδε, ἄξιον ὄντα τοῦ πιστεύεσθαι παρὰ τῆς σῆς φρονήσεως, διὰ τὸν φόβον τοῦ Κυρίου, CXLII 235 B, and also XCIV 187 C, CCXXV 344 D; and once to a laywoman, ἃ καὶ τὴν σὴν φρόνησιν ἐνθυμουμένην πράως ἔχειν ἐπὶ τῷ συμβάντι παρακαλοῦμεν, CCLXIX 415 C.

It occurs also in the following instances: to priests, ἴσθω σου τοῦτο ἡ φρόνησις, Isidorus V 319, 1521 A, and Basil CLVI 245 C; to a priestess, ἐδεξάμην ὅσα ἐπέστειλεν ἡ σὴ φρόνησις ἀγαθὰ καὶ καλὰ παρὰ τῶν θεῶν ἡμῖν ἐπαγγέλματα καὶ δῶρα, Julian XXXIV; to an unknown person, Athanasius 25 375 A.

χρηστότης: n., *Benignity.*

As a title, χρηστότης is found only in Athanasius and Basil. It is addressed to bishops and laymen of distinction.

The passages in which the title occurs for bishops are as follows: οὐδὲ ἡ ὑμετέρα χρηστότης ἀγνοεῖ, quoted in Athanasius 26 792 A; σφόδρα ἠθυμήσαμεν μὴ καταλαβόντες σου τὴν χρηστότητα, Basil CXXVI 217 C. Cf. also Athanasius 25 353 B, 372 C, 373 A, 396 A, and 26 796 B, 808 A; Basil XXIV 102 D, CLXXXI 265 D.

Χρηστότης is addressed to laymen in the following instances: οἶδε δέ σου ἡ χρηστότης, Athanasius 25 392 A; ἐσπεύσαμεν παρακαλέσαι τὴν χρηστότητά σου, μὴ ἐᾶσαι προβῆναι τοῖς ἀδικεῖν ἐπιχειροῦσι τὴν ἐπήρειαν, Basil CCCIII 440 B. Cf. also Athanasius 25 389 D; Basil XVII 96 A, LVI 150 E, LXXIII 167 A, LXXXIII 176 B, CIX 202 B, CXLIX 239 A.

The title also occurs in the following unaddressed letters of Basil: XXXVI 114 B, CCCX 443 B, CCCXVI 445 B.

TITLES FOR BISHOPS, LAYMEN, AND WOMEN

Several titles of this ecclesiastical-secular group were addressed sometimes to women.

σεμνοπρέπεια : n., *Reverence.*

This title is generally used in addressing laymen of high official rank and laywomen. It is found also for bishops. Examples occur in Synesius, Theodoret, and the Cappadocians.

The passages in which it occurs for laymen are as follows: πλὴν ἀλλ' ἐπειδὴ βούλομαι γενέσθαι χρήσιμος τῷ ἀνδρί, ἱκετεύω σου τὴν σεμνοπρέπειαν, Basil CXLIX 239 A; εἰ τοῦ Θεοδώρου μνήμη παρὰ τῇ σεμνοπρεπείᾳ τῇ σῇ, πῶς δὲ οὐ μέλλει, Synesius XXI 1353 D; cf. also Basil CXXVII 218 C, CXXXVII 228 D, CCXIV 321 A, CCCI 437 D.

The following examples are addressed to laywomen: ἐξέπεμψα πρὸς τὴν σὴν σεμνοπρέπειαν, Basil X 92 B; παρακαλῶ σου τὴν σεμνοπρέπειαν, Theodoret VIII 1181 A. Cf. Basil X 92 C; Theodoret VII 1180 D, XIV 1188 A, LXIX 1237 B, 1237 D, C 1293 B.

The Cappadocians use it as a title for bishops: ὅταν δὲ πάλιν πρὸς τὴν σὴν ἀπίδωμεν σεμνοπρέπειαν ..., Basil LXXXII 175 B; ἐξέπεμψα πρὸς τὴν σὴν σεμνοπρέπειαν, Gregory of Nyssa XXI 2; cf. also Gregory of Nazianzus XLII [8] 88 B, CCII 332 B.

There is one case in which the addressee is not known to us: Synesius CXXX 1513 C.

σεμνότατος : adj., *most revered.*

The adjective σεμνότατος is found as a title for bishops and for women. It occurs in Athanasius, Basil, Gregory of Nyssa, and Nilus.

We have found σεμνότατος in the following instances used as a title for bishops: ἐκ τῆς τοῦ σεμνοτάτου Γεωργίου συνουσίας, letter of Constantius quoted in Athanasius 25 637 A; ὃς ἐπανελθὼν διηγήσατο ἡμῖν τὰς ἐπὶ τοῦ σεμνοτάτου ἐπισκόπου Δαμάσου πρὸς τὴν σὴν τιμιότητα γενομένας αὐτῷ διαλέξεις, Basil CCLXVI 412 E; cf. also Athanasius 25 633 C, 636 C.

---

[8] Letter XLII is found also as XLVII among the letters of St. Basil.

Women are addressed with σεμνοτάτη as follows: ἐμὸς γάρ ἐστιν ἴδιος ὁ τῆς σεμνοτάτης μητρὸς ἡμῶν Παλλαδίας οἶκος, Basil CXXXVII 228 E; cf. also Gregory of Nyssa III 1; Nilus II 60, 225 D.

σεμνότης: n., *august Reverence.*

The title σεμνότης is addressed to bishops, to laymen of distinction, and to laywomen. St. Basil uses it frequently, but there is only one example of its occurrence elsewhere in the literature examined: ἐδεξάμην παρὰ τῆς σεμνότητός σου ἐπιστολήν, addressed to Athanasius in the *Apologia contra Arianos, 25* 368 A.

Basil addresses it to laymen as follows: πρὸς οὖν ταῦτα πάντα τὴν σὴν σεμνότητα παρακαλοῦμεν στῆναι, XXXII 112 B; ὅμως δὲ ἐκεῖνο βούλομαι πεπεῖσθαι τὴν σεμνότητά σου, CCXIV 323 A; cf. also CXLVIII 238 C, CLXIII 254 A, CLXXV 262 D, CLXXVIII 264 B, CLXXX 265 B, CCXIV 320 E, CCLXXII 418 B, CCLXXVII 421 C, CCCI 437 C, CCCXIII 444 C.

There are the following instances of its being addressed to **women**: ταῦτα οὖν ἔδει ἐπισταλῆναί σου τῇ σεμνότητι, CCXCVI 454 A; ἐπειδὴ εὗρον πρέπουσαν διάκονον τῶν πρὸς τὴν σὴν σεμνότητα γραμμάτων, CCXCVII 434 C; cf. also CCLXIX 415 B.

In the following passages, σεμνότης is used as a title for bishops: εἴπερ οὖν ὅλως ἀνέχεται καταβῆναι πρὸς τὴν ταπείνωσιν ἡμῶν ἡ σεμνότης σου, LX 155 B; ἐγνώρισα ταῦτα τῇ σεμνότητί σου, CXX 212 B; cf. also XCV 189 C, C 195 E, CXXVII 218 D, CXCI 284 C, CCII 299 A, CCXLIII 375 E.

The following are examples of σεμνότης addressed to persons who are unknown: Basil CI 197 A, CXIV 207 B, CCCIX 442 E, CCCXXV 449 D.

TITLES FOR PERSONS OF ALL CLASSES

The titles which were terms of courteous address to persons of any class are these:

γνησιώτατος: adj., *most true, most sincere.*

Γνησιώτατος is one of the more uncommon titles of esteem. It is addressed to all classes of persons.

It is given to bishops: ἐπείχθητε πρὸς ἡμᾶς, ἐπείχθητε ἤδη, ναὶ δεόμεθα, ἀδελφοὶ γνησιώτατοι, Basil XCII 185 C ; ἐρρωμένος, ὑπερευχόμενος ἡμῶν διατελοίης, δέσποτα θεοφιλέστατε καὶ ὁσιώτατε, καὶ πάντων ἐμοὶ γνησιώτατε ἀδελφέ, John of Antioch IV 173 B. Basil uses it once in referring to a priest: αὐτοῦ οὖν τούτου ἕνεκεν ἀπεστείλαμεν τὸν εὐλαβέστατον καὶ γνησιώτατον ἀδελφὸν ὑμῶν καὶ συνεργὸν τοῦ εὐαγγελίου Μελέτιον τὸν συμπρεσβύτερον, CCXXVI 346 A. There are two in-stances of its application to laymen: τοὺς τοῦ γνησιωτάτου καὶ τιμιω-τάτου υἱοῦ ἡμῶν Νικοβούλου παῖδας, Gregory of Nazianzus CLXXIV 285 B ; τοῦ ὑμετέρου μὲν γαμβροῦ, ἐμοῦ δὲ γνησιωτάτου φίλου τὴν τελευ-τήν, Theodoret XII 1185 A. It also occurs with reference to the clergy: ἐρχομένων τῶν γνησιωτάτων ἀδελφῶν τῶν περὶ Δομνῖνον πρὸς τὴν εὐλάβειάν σου, ἡδέως τὴν ἀφορμὴν τῶν γραμμάτων ἐδεξάμεθα, Basil CCLXIV 407 E ; cf. also Basil LVII 151 D, CCXXVI 345 E. Twice it occurs for persons who are not identified: Gregory of Nazi-anzus XCI 165 B ; Synesius CXXIII 1504 B.

διάθεσις : n., *Disposition.*

This title is used for all classes of persons. The examples of its occurrence are fairly numerous. There are several authors, how-ever, who do not make use of it; they are Gregory of Nazianzus, Gregory of Nyssa, Cyril of Alexandria, Isidorus, and Theodoret. It occurs once in Julian.

Athanasius addresses it to the emperor: καὶ περὶ ἡμῶν ἠξίου γράφειν πρὸς τὴν σὴν ἀδελφικὴν διάθεσιν, καὶ παρόντας μὲν ἐτίμα πολλάκις, καὶ ἀπόντας δὲ μετεπέμπετο, 25 604 B.

Διάθεσις occurs not infrequently in addressing bishops: τὰ γράμματα τῆς σῆς ἱερᾶς διαθέσεως ἀπεδόθη μοι ἐν τῇ ἐρήμῳ, Athanasius 26 529 A ; καὶ νῦν ἔμελλόν τινα ἀποστέλλειν αὐτοῦ τούτου ἕνεκεν, ὥστε γνωρίσαι ἡμῖν τὰ περὶ τῆς διαθέσεώς σου, Basil CC 298 A ; παρακαλῶ σοῦ τὴν διάθεσιν, John of Antioch I 1452 B. Cf. also Athanasius 25 353 C, and 26 529 A, 797 A ; Basil CLIV 243 D, CCLX 395 D ; Chrysostom XXVII 627, LXXXVIII 655, CXLII 697, CLX 705 ; John of Antioch I 1450 A ; Nestorius 56 C.

There are several examples of its use as a title for women: τὸ μὲν ἀκόλουθον ἦν καὶ ὀφειλόμενόν σου τῇ διαθέσει, ἡμᾶς αὐτοὺς παρεῖναι καὶ συμμετέχειν τῶν γινομένων, Basil CCLXIX 415 B ; πολὺ δὲ ἐξεπλάγην καὶ τὸ σόν, ὅτι τετάρτην ταύτην ἐπιστολὴν ἢ καὶ πέμπτην ἐπεσταλκὼς τῇ διαθέσει σου καὶ τῇ κοσμιότητι, μίαν ἐδεξάμην καὶ μόνην, Chrysostom

CXX 675; cf. also Chrysostom XLIII 633, LII 637, LXXVII 650, CLXIX 709.

The title occurs also in the following instances: to a deacon, . . . τὸ τῆς σῆς κεχωρίσθαι γλυκύτητος καὶ τῆς γνησίας καὶ εἰλικρινοῦς διαθέσεως, Chrysostom LXVII 645; to monks, τῇ μὲν ὑμετέρᾳ διαθέσει πεισθείς, καὶ πολλάκις παρ' ὑμῶν προτραπείς, ἔγραψα, Athanasius 25 692 A; to laymen, ἵν' οὖν μὴ παρ' ἑτέρων, ἀλλὰ καὶ παρὰ τῆς γλυκείας καὶ ποθεινο-τάτης ἡμῖν διαθέσεως ταῦτα μανθάνομεν, Chrysostom XLI 632, and τῇ σῇ διαθέσει δῶρον δίδωμι, Julian XXV.

In the following passages, the station in life of the addressee is not known: Athanasius 25 420 A, 480 A; Synesius XCVIII 1468 B.

It is sometimes difficult to determine whether or not διάθεσις should be interpreted as a title; for example, Chrysostom CXXX 689, 690, CCXIV 729.

ἐμμέλεια: n., *Grace.*

This title is used in addressing all classes of persons. It appears frequently in St. John Chrysostom, but we have found only one other example: i. e., ὥστε οὐ διδασκαλίας ἕνεκεν τοὺς λόγους τούτους ποιεῖσθαι ἡμᾶς νομίζειν προσῆκειν, οὐδὲ τοῦ ὑπομνῆσαι ὑμῶν τὴν ἐμμέλειαν, Basil CCXLIII 374 B, to the bishops of Italy and Gaul.

Chrysostom uses ἐμμέλεια as a title for bishops in the following passages: εἰ γὰρ καὶ πολλῷ τῷ μήκει τῆς ἐμμελείας ὑμῶν ἀπῳκίσθημεν, CXIII 669; cf. also 536, XXVI 626, CXLII 696.

Ἐμμέλεια is also given to priests: καὶ ἐπεστάλκαμεν πολλάκις πρὸς τὴν σὴν ἐμμέλειαν, CI 661; cf. also XLV 634, CXXX 689, CXLV 698, CCXXII 734.

It occurs once in a letter to a deacon: ἡ μακρά σου τῆς ἐμμελείας σιγή, LXVII 645.

It is addressed also to laymen of high station: μέλλων ἐπιστέλλειν ὑμῶν τῇ ἐμμελείᾳ, CXXVIII 688; οὐδὲ μικρὸν τῷ μήκει τῆς ὁδοῦ διειρ-γόμεθα τῆς ἐμμελείας τῆς ὑμετέρας, CXXIX 688; cf. also CXXVII 688, CLXXXVII 717, CCIV 725, CCXVI 730, CCXXIII 734, CCXXVIII 737.

There are several instances of the use of ἐμμέλεια as a title for women: for deaconesses, διὸ παρακαλῶ σου τὴν ἐμμέλειαν μηδένα λοιπὸν ἀποστέλλειν ἐνταῦθα, XV 620 and also II 556, VI 601, CLXXXV

716; for laywomen of rank, . . . ἀγάπην, ἣν ἀεὶ περὶ τὴν σὴν ἐμμέλειαν ἐπεδειξάμην ἀκμάζουσαν, CXXXIII 692, and also XVIII 623, XXXII 628, LII 637, CV 664, CLXVIII 709, CCXXIX 737, CCXXXI 737, 738, CCXXXII 738, 739.

In the following instances, the addressee is not identified: LI 636, LXIII 643, CXXXIV 692, CXLIV 697, 698, CLXXVII 712, CLXXXVI 716, CCV 726.

κεφαλή : n., friend, sir.

Κεφαλή is used as a title of address for persons of all classes, usually indicating a friendly relation between the writer of the letter and the addressee. It never appears without a qualifying adjective except in Libanius. It occurs most frequently in the expression ὦ φίλη κεφαλή, and also joined with the adjectives, ἱερά and θεία.

The examples are as follows:

To bishops: ἀπόδος τοίνυν, ὦ φιλη κεφαλή, ἐπιστὰς ἡμῶν τῇ πατρίδι, Basil CXVIII 210 B; ἀλλὰ κρατείτω καὶ νῦν ὅ τι ἂν δόξειε τῇ πατρικῇ σου κεφαλῇ, Synesius LXVII 1417 B; ἴστω τοίνυν ἡ ἱερά σου καὶ θεοφιλὴς κεφαλή, ὡς οὐδεὶς ἡμῶν ἀκήκοε πώποτε δύο κηρυττόντων υἱούς, Theodoret CIV 1297 B. Cf. also Basil XXV 103 D, CXCVIII 290 B; Gregory of Nazianzus XLVI 96 A, LVIII 117 B; Synesius LXVII 1413 B, 1417 B, 1432 B; Isidorus I 84, 241 A; II 21, 472 A; III 130, 829 C; Alypius 145 D; John of Antioch II 132 C, V 248 B; Theodoret XI 1184 C, XII 1185 A, XVI 1193 B, XXIV 1205 B, XLVII 1224 D, LX 1232 C, CII 1296 B, CXIII 1317 C, CXXII 1333 B, CXXX 1344 A.

To other members of the clergy: to an archimandrite, τὴν θεοφιλῆ σου περιπτυσσόμενοι κεφαλήν, Theodoret CXLI 1365 D; to priests, ἡμᾶς δὲ νόμιζε, τιμία κεφαλή, Basil CLVI 245 B, and Theodoret XXX 1208 D, LXI 1233 A, CVII 1301 A; to deacons, οὐκ ἔστιν, ὦ φίλη κεφαλή, μηχανὴν εὑρεῖν, Isidorus II 76, 517 C, and III 267, 948 B; to a monk, ὦ φίλη μου κεφαλή, Theodoret CXLII 1368 D.

To laymen: ἐλθὲ οὖν, ὦ φίλη κεφαλή, φέρων ἡμῖν ἀγαθῶν πλῆθος, σαυτόν, Gregory of Nyssa XII 4; τῷ ὄντι γὰρ ἤλγησα τὴν ψυχήν, τῆς φίλης ἐμοὶ κεφαλῆς τὴν ἐκδημίαν μεμαθηκώς, Theodoret LXIX 1237 D. Cf. also Basil XCIX 195 A, CXII 204 C; Gregory of Nyssa IV 10; Synesius LXXIX 1452 A, CLIV 1557 B; Chrysostom XXIV 626,

LVIII 641, XCV 659; Theodoret X 1184 A, XIV 1188 A, XXI 1201 B, LVIII 1229 D. Julian has the following examples: νῦν δή σοι δῶρον, ὦ φίλη κεφαλή, δίδωμι μικρὸν μὲν ὅπερ ἐστί . . . , XXV; also LXXXIII.

In the following instances, the station in life of the person to whom the title is addressed is not known: Basil VIII [9] 81 C, CCCVII 442 A; Gregory of Nazianzus XXXII 72 C; Synesius XXXVII 1364 A, XLIX 1377 A, LVI 1381 D, LXXI 1433 D, LXXXV 1456 A, XCV 1465 A, CIX 1492 B, CXXIII 1504 A, 1504 B, CXXVI 1505 C, CXXXII 1518 C, CXXXVIII 1529 B, CXLII 1536 B, 1537 A, CXLVIII 1549 D, CL 1552 C; Theodoret I 1173 B, II 1176 B.

κύριος: n., *Lord, Sir.*

The title κύριος is addressed most frequently to bishops. It is found rarely for members of the lower clergy, except in the letters of John Chrysostom who makes frequent use of it in addressing priests. Athanasius addresses it twice to the emperor. As a title for the laity, κύριος is common for persons of distinction and, in Gregory of Nazianzus, it occurs for members of his family.[10] Κύριος appears also in the letters of Cyril of Alexandria and Theodoret, and several minor authors, but we find no examples in Basil, Gregory of Nyssa, and Isidorus.

The early examples of its occurrence are as follows: σὺ οὖν, κύριε υἱέ, προηγουμένως πρόσεχε τῇ τῶν θείων Γραφῶν ἀναγνώσει, Origen to Gregory Thaumaturgus, 92 A and also 88 A; χαῖρε, κύριέ μου, καὶ υἱέ, καὶ πάντων τιμιώτατε Ὠρίγενες, παρὰ Ἀφρικανοῦ, Sextus Julius Africanus 41 D; . . . δι' ὧν σὲ ἐγνώρισα, τὸν κατὰ πάντα ἄριστον καὶ κύριόν μου καὶ ἀδελφόν, Alexander of Jerusalem to Origen quoted in Eusebius H. E. VI 14, 9.

It is addressed to bishops in the following passages: κύριέ μου ποθεινότατε, Athanasius 26 1180 B; ὁ κύριός μου καὶ θεοφιλέστατος Ἑλλάδιος ὁ ἐπίσκοπος, Gregory of Nazianzus CLXXXIII 300 A; εὐθὺς καὶ παραχρῆμα ἀπεστείλαμεν τὸν κύριόν μου, καὶ κατὰ πάντα θεοφιλέστατον καὶ ἁγιώτατον ἐπίσκοπον Παῦλον, John of Antioch IV 172 A.

---

[9] Letter VIII probably belongs to Evagrius of Pontus; cf. p. 79, note 5.
[10] Cf. the corresponding use of κυρία, p. 78.

Cf. also Athanasius *25* 221 A, 240 A, 353 B, 356 A, 364 C, 368 A.
368 B, 388 B, 389 B, 393 B, 393 D, 396 A, and *26* 1049 A, 1180 A;
Arius quoted in Theodoret H. E. I 5, 1; Theophilus 61 B; Gregory
of Nazianzus CXXXIX 236 B, CLXII 268 C, CLXXXII 296 C,
CLXXXIII 300 B, 300 C, 301 A; Chrysostom 529, 534, 535, XI
609, XII 609, 610, XIV 612, 613, XXXVII 630, XXXVIII 631,
LXXXVII 654, CXXVI 687, CCIV 725, CCXXI 733; Cyril of
Alexandria XIII 96 A, XVI 104 A, 104 C, XXIII 133 D, XXXIX
173 C, 176 A, 176 C, XL 181 D, XLII 221 C, XLVIII 249 B,
L 276 C, LXXII 344 D, 345 C, 345 D, LXXVII 360 B, LXXXV
376 C, 377 A; John of Antioch I 1452 C, 1457 A, II 132 B, 132 C,
V 248 A, 248 B; Theodoret XLIII 1220 D, LI 1228 A, LII 1228 C,
LXXXI 1261 A, LXXXIII 1268 D, LXXXVI 1277 C, XCII
1285 D, XCIII 1288 B, CX 1305 B, CXI 1308 B, 1308 C, CXIII
1316 B, CXXI 1332 A, CXLIV 1373 C, CXLVII 1409 C.

The following examples are addressed to priests: παρὰ τῶν κυρίων
μου τῶν συμπρεσβυτέρων, Gregory of Nazianzus CLII 257 C; πάντα
γὰρ εἶπον τῷ κυρίῳ μου τῷ τιμιωτάτῳ καὶ εὐλαβεστάτῳ πρεσβυτέρῳ Κων-
σταντίῳ Chrysostom LIV 639; κύριέ μου τιμιώτατε, Chrysostom
CXXVI 686; cf. also Chrysostom XIII 611, XXI 624, XXII 624,
625, XXIII 625, XXV 626, XXVI 626, LIII 637, LX 642, LXII
643, LXXIX 651, XCVII 660, CXXIII 677, CXXVI 686, 687,
CLV 703, CLVI 703, CLVII 704, CLVIII 704, CLIX 705, CLX
705, CLXI 706, CLXII 706, CLXIII 707, CLXIV 707, CLXV
708, CLXVI 708, CLXVII 709, CLXXV 711, CCXXIV 735.

There are the following instances for other members of the lower
clergy: to a priest and deacon, οἱ μέντοι κύριοί μου, ὁ εὐλαβέστατος
πρεσβύτερος Ἰωάννης, καὶ ὁ τιμιώτατος Παῦλος ὁ διάκονος ἐλαυνόμενοι
πανταχόθεν, Chrysostom CXLVIII 700; to deacons, κύριός μου καὶ
ἀδελφὸς ἱερὸς Ἀμβρόσιος, Origen 85 C; πολλὰ παραγγείλαντες τῷ κυρίῳ
μου τῷ εὐλαβεστάτῳ διακόνῳ Θεοδότῳ, Chrysostom LXI 643, and
XLIII 633, LXVII 645; to a lector, τὸν κύριόν μου τὸν τιμιώτατον τὸν
ἀναγνώστην Θεόδοτον παρακατατίθεμαί σου τῇ εὐλαβείᾳ, Chrysostom
CXXXV 693; to the ascetic Jacob, τὸν γνήσιον αὐτοῦ δοῦλον, τὸν
ἁγιώτατον ἄνθρωπον τοῦ Θεοῦ τὸν κύριον Ἰάκωβον, Theodoret XLIV
1221 D and XLII 1220 B. Cyril of Alexandria addresses it to an
archimandrite: τῷ κυρίῳ Δαλματίῳ XXIII 132 D. For the clergy,

cf. also Alexander of Jerusalem quoted in Eusebius H. E. VI 11, 6;
Chrysostom CXVIII 673.

The two instances of its use as a title of the emperor are as
follows: κύριε θεοφιλέστατε βασιλεῦ, letter of bishops in Athanasius
26 792 B and 792 C.

There are many examples of κύριος addressed to laymen of dis-
tinction: τῷ κυρίῳ μου Θεοδώρῳ τῷ ἐπαρχικῷ, τῷ ἀγαγόντι ἡμᾶς εἰς τὴν
Κουκουσόν, Chrysostom CXV 671; ὁ κύριός μου, ὁ μεγαλοπρεπέστατος
καὶ ἐνδοξότατος κώμης, Cyril of Alexandria XXVIII 145 A; ἐβεβαίωσε
δὲ ὁ ἐνδοξότατος καὶ φιλόχριστος κυρίος Φλωρέντιος, Theodoret XLVII
1225 A. Cf. Athanasius 25 385 A, 393 D; Chrysostom VIII 607,
XII 610, XIV 613, 615, 616, LXV 644, C 661, CCXI 728,
CCXXIX 737, CCXXX 737, CCXXXI 738, CCXXXII 738,
CCXXXIX 745; John of Antioch I 1450 A, IV 172 A, V 248 C;
Cyril of Alexandria XXXVII 168 C, 169 B, XL 184 C, XLVIII
249 B, 252 C; Theodoret XLIV 1221 B, XCVII 1292 A.

Gregory of Nazianzus addresses it to members of his family:
τὸν μὲν οὖν κύριον τὸν πατέρα ἡμῶν, VII 33 A; τῶν κυρίων μου τῶν
ἀνεψιῶν, XIV 45 C; τοὺς κυρίους μου τοὺς ἀνεψιοὺς Ἑλλάδιον καὶ
Εὐλάλιον, XV 48 C.

The following examples are addressed to persons whose station
in life is not known: Chrysostom XXXV 630, XLIV 634, XLIX
635, CLXXVII 712; Theodoret CXXX 1348 C.

ποθεινότατος: adj., most dear; as a substantive, most dear friend.

The title ποθεινότατος is addressed to persons of all classes. There
are examples of its use in Athanasius, Basil, Gregory of Nyssa,
Cyril of Alexandria, and John Chrysostom. The pagan Julian also
makes use of it.

Ποθεινότατος is addressed to bishops in the following passages:
ἀγαπητοῖς καὶ ποθεινοτάτοις ἀδελφοῖς ἐν Κυρίῳ χαίρειν, Athanasius 25
252 B; ἔρρωσθαί σε ἐν Κυρίῳ, ἀγαπητὲ καὶ ποθεινότατε ἀδελφέ, Theophilus 61 C; πέπεισο γάρ, τιμιώτατέ μοι καὶ ποθεινότατε ὡς ἀληθῶς, ὅτι
πόλλων εἰς πεῖραν ἐλθὼν ὁ παρ' ἡμῖν λαός, Basil CLXXVI 263 B. Cf.
also Arius quoted in Theodoret H. E. I 5, 1; Theophilus 61 C;
Serapion 925 A; Athanasius 25 240 A, 308 C, 389 B, and 26 529 A,
796 A, 796 B, 1049 A, 1069 B, 1073 A, 1080 C, 1084 B, 1180 A,
1180 B; Basil CXXX 222 A, 223 A, CCXLIII 372 D, CCXLV

382 D, CCLXV 411 E, CCLXVI 411 E, CCCLXIV 465 E, 466 D; Chrysostom XI 609; Cyril of Alexandria XVI 104 A, LXXXIV 385 B.

The title occurs frequently for members of the lower clergy. It is addressed to priests in the following instances: ἐρρῶσθαι ὑμᾶς ἐν Κυρίῳ εὔχομαι, ἀγαπητοὶ καὶ ποθεινότατοι υἱοί, Athanasius 26 1168 B; ... ἔκ τε τῶν γραμμάτων ἃ ἐπεστείλατε ἡμῖν διὰ τῶν ποθεινοτάτων συμπρεσβυτέρων ἡμῶν, Basil CCLXIII 404 E; ὁ ποθεινότατος καὶ γλυκύτατος Ἰωάννης ὁ πρεσβύτερος, Chrysostom LV 640. Cf. also Basil LXXXVI 178 E, CXX 211 D, CXXI 212 D, CXXXII 225 A, CXCVII 288 E, CCIII 302 D, CCXV 323 B, CCXX 333 C, CCXXXIX 367 C, CCXL 369 B, CCXLV 382 D, CCL 385 A, CCLIII 389 B, CCLIV 389 D, CCLV 390 B, CCLVI 390 C, 391 B; Chrysostom LIII 638, CCXXX 737. It is used in addressing deacons, ὁ ποθεινότατος υἱὸς Δωρόθεος ὁ συνδιάκονος, Basil CLVI 246 C and CCLXV 409 A; and also in addressing a lector, τὸν ποθεινότατον ἀδελφὸν Εὐσέβιον τὸν ἀναγνώστην, Basil CXCVIII 290 A.

Monks are addressed with ποθεινότατος as follows: ὦ ἀγαπητὲ καὶ ποθεινότατε Ὠρσίσιε, Athanasius 26 980 A; μακάριοί ἐστε ἐν ἡμέρᾳ κρίσεως, ποθεινότατοι, Serapion 937 D. Cf. also Athanasius 25 692 A, and 26 977 C, 980 A, 980 C, 1185 A; Cyril of Alexandria I 9 A, XIX 128 C, XXVI 140 C, 141 C, LV 289 D.

For clergy, cf. also Cyril of Alexandria XXIII 132 D.

It occurs also in addressing churches: ἀγαπητοῖς καὶ ποθεινοτάτοις ἀδελφοῖς ἐν Κυρίῳ χαίρειν, Athanasius 25 352 A; ὑμῖν γὰρ ἐπιτρέπω, ποθεινότατοι ἀδελφοί, Basil CCIV 306 A; Κύριλλος πρεσβυτέροις καὶ διακόνοις καὶ λαῷ Ἀλεξανδρείας, ἀγαπητοῖς καὶ ποθεινοτάτοις ἐν Κυρίῳ χαίρειν, Cyril of Alexandria XX 128 D. Cf. also Basil CCXXI 334 B; Cyril of Alexandria XVIII 124 A, XX 129 B, XXI 129 C, 132 A, XXIV 137 A, 157 C, 137 D.

Ποθεινότατος appears also as a title for laymen in the following passages: τῷ ἀγαπητῷ καὶ ἀληθῶς ποθεινοτάτῳ υἱῷ Μαξίμῳ φιλοσόφῳ, Athanasius 26 1085 A; διόπερ χρῇζων δυσωπῆσαι τὸν ποθεινότατον υἱὸν Καλλισθένην ἡγησάμην, Basil LXXII 166 B; κύριοί μου ποθεινότατοι καὶ τιμώτατοι, Chrysostom C 661. Cf. also Basil CLXXVIII 264 C, CC 298 A, CCXI 318 A; Chrysostom VIII 607, XLI 632, CCXXIX 737, CCXXX 737, CCXXXII 738. Julian has several examples:

ἀδελφὲ ποθεινότατε καὶ φιλικώτατε, I; ἔρρωσό μοι, ἀδελφὲ ποθεινότατε καὶ προσφιλέστατε, LIII; cf. also V, VII, LII.

The following examples are uncertain: Basil CCXCV 433 B, Gregory of Nyssa VIII 4, Chrysostom CCXIX 732.

σοφός: adj., *wise;* as a substantive, *my wise friend.*

The adjective σοφός appears to be used by Isidorus as a title for persons of all classes. There is one example in Gregory of Nazianzus. The pagan Libanius also makes use of it.

The examples are as follows: to laymen, ἀλλ', ὦ σοφέ, πάλιν ἂν εἶπε πρὸς αὐτόν, εὖ μὲν λέγεις, Isidorus II 146, 600 D and also II 103, 545 D; 279, 709 C; 288, 717 C; III 389, 1029 C; IV 43, 1093 C; 85, 1145 C; 171, 1264 A; V 250, 1481 D; 412, 1572 B; to bishops, ὦ σοφέ, II 198, 644 B and V 318, 1520 D; to priests, εἰ ὁ πηλὸς ἐξυμώθη καὶ νέον φύραμα γέγονεν, ὦ σοφοί, Gregory of Nazianzus CI 185 C and also Isidorus III 311, 977 B; IV 175, 1265 C; to deacons, ἔχε, ὦ σοφέ, τὴν γνώμην εὐγνώμονα, III 174, 865 and IV 127, 1204 C; V 369, 1548 C; to a monk, ὦ σοφέ, IV 36, 1088 C; to unknown persons, II 8, 464 C; III 135, 833 D; V 202, 1453 D. Cf. also Libanius, τὸν σοφὸν Ἰάμβλιχον, ϧπβ′ 1, ‚αια′ 1, ‚αλε′ 4, ‚αλη′ 2.

σοφώτατος: adj., *most wise;* as a substantive, *most wise sir.*

The adjective σοφώτατος is used in addressing persons of all classes. Isidorus alone makes frequent use of it, but there are occasional examples in Gregory of Nazianzus, Synesius, Theodoret, and Procopius. Σοφώτατος is recorded as a title in papyri of the fourth and fifth centuries.[11] The earliest example that we have found occurs in Eusebius and is addressed to the emperor: ὁ μὲν σοφώτατος ἡμῶν καὶ εὐσεβέστατος βασίλευς τὰ τοιαῦτα διεφιλοσόφει, quoted in Theodoret H. E. I 12, 7.

Σοφώτατος is addressed to bishops in the following instances: βαθύ σε γῆρας καὶ λιπαρὸν περιμείνειεν ἁγιώτατε καὶ σοφώτατε, Synesius IX 1345 C. Cf. also Isidorus III 21, 745 C; 46, 761 C; 186, 876 A; 330, 988 D.

Isidorus also gives the title to priests: ὦ σοφώτατε, κινδυνεύεις

---

[11] Moulton and Milligan s. v.; Preisigke s. v.

ἀγνοεῖν, II 46, 488 A; cf. also III 18, 744 C; 248, 928 A; 340, 1000 C; V 167, 1424 C.

It occurs for deacons as follows: ἐπέσκηψεν ὁ σοφώτατος ἀρχιδιάκονος, Theodoret CXLVI 1389 D; ὦ σοφώτατε, Isidorus III 168, 860 D; 403, 1037 C; IV 173, 1264 D.

Laymen are addressed with σοφώτατος as follows: τί γὰρ παθών, ὦ σοφώτατε, Gregory of Nazianzus XI 41 B; ἀνέγνων τὸν λόγον, σοφώτατε, καὶ ὑπερτεθαύμακα, Basil CCCLIII 461 A, a letter which is considered spurious; cf. also Isidorus III 380, 1025 A; V 5, 1328 B.

The title is addressed to persons who are unidentified in the following instances: Isidorus I 181, 300 C; V 286, 1504 A; V 310, 1516 D; Procopius XLIV 2753 C, XCIII 2789 B.

τιμιότης: n., *Honor.*

Τιμιότης is addressed to persons of every class. It is a favorite title with Basil and John Chrysostom. There are several examples in Gregory of Nazianzus, but only one in Athanasius, Gregory of Nyssa, and Cyril of Alexandria. The title does not occur in Synesius, Nilus, Isidorus, and Theodoret. Τιμιότης is noted as a common form of address in papyri.[12]

It is addressed to bishops as follows: τὰ παρόντα ταῦτα γράμματα πρὸς τὴν σὴν τιμιότητα στεῖλαι ἔκρινα, addressed to Athanasius in 25 624 B; ὃς ὁποῖα μὲν κάμνει, οὐδὲ τὴν σὴν ἔλαθε τιμιότητα, Basil XXXI 111 A; ἐπέσταλκα τῇ τιμιότητί σου, Chrysostom CXXXVIII 695. Cf. also Basil XLVIII 141 D, LIX 154 A, LX 155 A, LXVI 158 D, LXVII 160 C, LXVIII 161 A, LXIX 161 D, 162 A, LXXXIX 180 C, XC 182 C, XCV 189 A, XCVIII 192 C, CXVII 209 B, CXX 212 A, CXXXIII 225 C, CXXXVI 228 B, CXXXVIII 230 B, CCXLI 370 D, CCLXV 411 A, CCLXVI 413 A; Gregory of Nazianzus LXXVI 141 A; Gregory of Nyssa X 4; Chrysostom XXVII 627, XXX 628, CX 668, CXI 668, CXXXI 690, CXXXVIII 695, CL 701, CLXII 706, CLXIII 707, CLXIV 707, CLXVI 708, CLXXXIII 715; Cyril of Alexandria LXXXV 377 A.

Priests are addressed with τιμιότης chiefly in Chrysostom: ἐνέτυχου

---

[12] Moulton and Milligan s. v.

τοῖς ἀποσταλεῖσι βιβλίοις παρὰ τῆς τιμιότητός σου, Basil CXXXV
226 B; οὐ παύσομαι μακαρίζων σου τὴν τιμιότητα, Chrysostom CLXXX
713; διὸ καὶ προσαγορεύω σου τὴν τιμιότητα, Chrysostom CCXV 730.
Cf. also LIII 638, LXIX 646, LXXVIII 650, XCII 656, XCVII
660, CXXVI 686, 687, CLXXX 713, CCX 728, CCXIV 729,
CCXL [13] 746, CCXLI [13] 746.

Chrysostom gives the title once to a deacon: τῆς σῆς κεχωρισμένοι
τιμιότητος, CXXXV 693.

It occurs for monks as follows: πλάτανον τὴν χρυσῆν . . . ἣν ἐγὼ
ἐφύτευσα, Ἀπολλὼς ἐπότισεν, ἡ σὴ τιμιότης, ἀλλ᾽ ὁ Θεὸς ηὔξησεν, Gregory
of Nazianzus VI 32 A; διὰ τῶν γραμμάτων ἐσπούδακα ὑμῶν συγγενέσθαι
τῇ τιμιότητι, Chrysostom LVI 640; cf. also Chrysostom XXXVI 630.

Τιμιότης is frequent in Basil as a title for laymen of distinction:
ἔδωκαν μείζονα τὴν χάριν ἢ ἔλαβον οἱ πολῖται τῆς μητροπόλεως ἡμῶν
παρασχόμενοί μοι ἀφορμὴν τῶν πρὸς τὴν σὴν τιμιότητα γραμμάτων, Basil
XV 94 D; ἐπόθουν διὰ πολλοῦ προσειπεῖν σου τὴν τιμιότητα, Gregory of
Nazianzus CXXXVII 233 A; εἰ καὶ μὴ συνεχῶς ἐπεστάλκαμεν τῇ
τιμιότητί σου, Chrysostom XXXVIII 631. Cf. also Gregory of
Nazianzus CXXV 220 A, CCVIII 345 A; Basil LXXXIII 176 C,
LXXXVI 178 D, XCIV 187 C, XCIX 193 A, CII 198 B, CVI
200 D, CXLII 235 B, CXLIII 235 D, CLV 244 C, 244 D,
CLXXVIII 264 A, CCXI 318 A, CCXIV 321 A, CCXC 428 C,
CCCIII 440 A, CCCVI 441 A, 441 C, CCCXI 443 C, CCCXIII
444 B, CCCXXVIII 450 D; Chrysostom CXCIII 720.

Only in John Chrysostom does τιμιότης appear as a title for
women. It is addressed to deaconesses as follows: μὴ δεξάμενος παρὰ
τῆς σῆς τιμιότητος ἐπιστολήν, σφόδρα ἤλγησα, X 609; παρακαλῶ σου τὴν
τιμιότητα, CIV 663; cf. also IV 590, 595, VI 599, VIII 607, IX 608,
XIV 616, CIII 662, CIV 664. There are the following examples
of its being addressed to laywomen: διὸ δὴ παρακαλοῦμεν τὴν τιμιότητά
σου, XXXIX 631; καὶ ἔμπροσθεν ἐπέσταλκά σου τῇ τιμιότητι, LXXVII
650; cf. also LVII 640, CXVII 672, CCXXXII 738, CCXXXII
739, CCXXXVII 743, CCXXXVIII 743.

In the following instances, the title is addressed to persons who
are unknown: Basil LXIV 157 C, LXXXVIII 179 E, CCXLIX
384 E, CCLXXV 420 D, CCCVIII 442 B, CCCXIV 444 D,

---

[13] Letters CCXL and CCXLI belong to the priest Constantius.

CCCXV 445 A, CCCXVII 445 D, CCCXX 446 A, 447 A, CCCXXII 447 A, 448 A, CCCXXVI 450 A; Gregory of Nazianzus III 24 B, CCXXX 373 A; Chrysostom XXIV 626, XLIX 636, LXXII 648, CXXII 676, CLXXVI 712.

τιμιώτατος: adj., *most honorable*; as a substantive, *most honorable sir*.

The title τιμιώτατος is used commonly in referring to persons of all classes. We have found examples in all authors of importance, except Gregory of Nyssa, Nilus, and Synesius. Τιμιώτατος is cited as frequent in papyri as a term of address.[14]

In the following passages, it occurs as a title for bishops: τῷ τιμιωτάτῳ ἀδελφῷ καὶ ὁμοψύχῳ ᾿Αλεξάνδρῳ, ᾿Αλέξανδρος ἐν Κυρίῳ χαίρειν, Alexander of Alexandria I 548 A; ἃ παρὰ τῶν κυρίων μου τῶν τιμιωτάτων ἐπισκόπων ἐπέσταλται πρὸς τὴν σὴν εὐλάβειαν, Gregory of Nazianzus CLXII 268 C; ὁ Θεὸς καὶ ὁ Κύριος ἡμῶν, τὴν ἁγίαν ὑμῶν σύνοδον φυλάξῃ, ὅπερ εὐχόμεθα, τιμιώτατοι ἀδελφοί, Cyril of Alexandria LXXXV 377 B. Cf. also Eusebius, letter to Flacillus, H. E. IV; Alexander of Alexandria II 572 A, 577 B; Athanasius 25 385 D, 388 B, and 26 700 C, 813 A; Basil LXVI 159 B, LXIX 162 B, LXX 163 D, XC 181 B, 181 D, XCI 182 E, CXXX 222 A, 223 A, CLXXVI 263 B, CXCVIII 290 B, CC 298 C, CCIII 300 C, 301 E, CCV 308 C, CCXLII 371 C, CCXLIII 373 B, CCXLIV 382 D, CCLVIII 392 E, 394 C, 395 A, CCLXIII 407 B, CCLXVI 411 E, 413 B, CCLXVII 414 A; Gregory of Nazianzus CLXXXIII 300 C, CLXXXIV 301 B; Chrysostom 529, 534, 536, XII 610, XXV 626, XXVI 626, XXVII 626, XXX 628, XXXVII 630, 631, XXXVIII 631, LXXXVII 654, LXXXVIII 655, CIX 667, CXII 669, CXXXI 690, CXLII 696, CLII 701, CLX 705, CLXII 706, CLXXXIV 716, CCXXX 737; Isidorus II 10, 465 B; Nestorius 57 B; Cyril of Alexandria XXIII 133 C, LXXXV 376 C, 377 A.

The title is applied to priests as follows: τῷ τιμιωτάτῳ καὶ θεοφιλεστάτῳ ἀδελφῷ καὶ συμπρεσβυτέρῳ Κληδονίῳ Γρηγόριος ἐν Κυρίῳ χαίρειν, Gregory of Nazianzus CI 176 A; οἶδας καὶ αὐτός κύριέ μου τιμιώτατε, ὅσον . . . , Chrysostom XCVII 660; ταῦτα διὰ τοῦ τιμιωτάτου καὶ εὐλαβεστάτου πρεσβυτέρου Στεφάνου γέγραφα, Theodoret LXXVII

---

[14] Moulton and Milligan s. v.

1252 B.   Cf. also Basil CCXL 369 B; Gregory of Nazianzus XVI
49 B, XLIII 89 B, CLXVIII 277 C, CLXIX 280 A, CLXX 280 B,
CCXI 348 C, CCXIX 357 B, CCXXI 361 A; Chrysostom 535,
XXII 624, XXIII 625, XXV 626, XXVII 626, LIII 637, LIV
639, LX 642, LXII 643, LXXVI 649, LXXVIII 650, LXXIX
651, CI 661, CXIV 670, 671, CXVIII 673, CXXVI 686, CXLIII
697, CLV 703, CLVI 703, CLVII 704, CLVIII 704, CLIX 705,
CLX 705, CLXI 706, CLXII 706, CLXIII 707, CLXIV 707,
CLXV 708, CLXVI 708, CLXVII 709, CLXXV 711, CCXVII
731, CCXXI 733, CCXXX 737, and the letter of Constantius
CCXL 746; Theodoret CXXXII 1349 D.

Τιμώτατος is also addressed to deacons: ὁ τιμιώτατος υἱὸς ἡμῶν
Γεώργιος, Gregory of Nazianzus CLI 257 A; μακαρίζομεν δὲ καὶ τοὺς
τιμιωτάτους διακόνους Εὐσέβιον καὶ Λαμπρότατον, Chrysostom CLXXX
714; ὁ τιμιώτατος καὶ εὐλαβέστατος διάκονος Θαλάσσιος, Theodoret
XXIV 1205 A.   Cf. also Chrysostom 530, XLIII 633, LXVII 645,
CXXXV 693, CXLVIII 700, CLXVIII 709; Theodoret XXXVII
1216 A, CXXXI 1348 D.

There are two instances of its being applied to lectors: τὸν κύριόν
μου τὸν τιμιώτατον τὸν ἀναγνώστην Θεόδοτον παρακατατίθεμαί σου τῇ
εὐλαβείᾳ, Chrysostom CXXXV 693; τὸν τιμιώτατον καὶ εὐλαβέστατον
Ὑπάτιον τὸν ἀναγνώστην, Theodoret XI 1184 C.

Monks are addressed with τιμιώτατος as follows: μακάριοι τοίνυν
ἐστὲ καὶ τρισμακάριοι, ὦ τιμιώτατοι Θεῷ μονάζοντες, Serapion 928 D; τοῖς
τιμιωτάτοις ἀδελφοῖς τοῖς ὑμετέροις τὴν ἐπιστολὴν δεδωκότες, Theodoret
CXLII 1365 D.   Cf. also Serapion 932 D, 936 D, 940 D, 941 B;
Basil CCXXVI 347 B.

Basil uses τιμιώτατος in addressing churches: ἐνέτυχον τοῖς γράμμασιν ὑμῶν, ἀδελφοὶ τιμιώτατοι, CCLXI 401 B; cf. also CCIV 302 E.

There are several instances of its use as a title for laymen: ἀντὶ
οὖν τῆς ἐπὶ τοῖς γράμμασιν εὐφροσύνης πολλὴν οἴδαμεν χάριν τῷ τιμιωτάτῳ
υἱῷ ἡμῶν Εὐφημίῳ, Basil CLIV 243 D; παρὰ τοῦ τιμιωτάτου τῶν οἰκείων
κόμητος, Gregory of Nazianzus CLI 257 A; δέσποτά μου τιμιώτατε,
Chrysostom CCIX 728.   Cf. also Athanasius 25 637 A; Basil
LXXIII 167 E, XCIX 195 A, CCXXX 353 D, CCLXXIX 422 E,
CCLXXXIV 424 E, CCCXLIV 457 E; Gregory of Nazianzus
XXII 57 A, XXIII 57 C, CXXXIV 229 B, CLVII 265 A,
CLXXIV 285 B, CCXXIV 368 C; Chrysostom XXXVIII 631,

XLVIII 635, LXV 644, LXXIII 648, LXXV 649, C 661, CLXXV 712, CCXI 728, CCXVI 730, CCXXXI 738, and the letter of Constantius, CCXXXIX 745.

It occurs also for women in the letters of Chrysostom: for deaconesses, δέσποινά μου τιμωτάτη καὶ εὐλαβεστάτη, CIII 663, and CXCI 718; for laywomen, κυρία μου τιμωτάτη, CLXXVIII 713, and CLXVIII 709.

The following are passages in which τιμώτατος is addressed to unidentified persons: Basil CCLXXIII 419 D; Gregory of Nazianzus CXLV 248 C, CCXI 348 C, CCXXI 361 B, CCXXVII 369 C; Chrysostom XXXI 628, XXXV 630, XLIV 634, 635, LI 636, CLXXVII 712.

υἱός: n., *son*.

As a title, υἱός is addressed to juniors in age, in ecclesiastical rank, or to lay persons. The term is one of familiar address.

It occurs once in the Epistles of the New Testament, ἀσπάζεται ὑμᾶς ἡ ἐν Βαβυλῶνι συνεκλεκτή, καὶ Μάρκος ὁ υἱός μου, I Peter V 13; and once in the Epistle of Pseudo-Barnabas, χαίρετε, υἱοὶ καὶ θυγατέρες, I 1.

The title is addressed to juniors in the following early examples: χαῖρε, κύριέ μου, καὶ υἱέ, καὶ πάντων τιμώτατε Ὠρίγενες, παρὰ Ἀφρικανοῦ, Sextus Julius Africanus 41 D; αἰδεσιμώτατε υἱὲ Γρηγόριε, Origen 88 A. Cf. also Origen 92 A; Dionysius of Alexandria 1272 B, 1288 C; Alexander to Athanasius, 25 368 A.

Bishops use υἱός in referring to priests, ἐρρῶσθαι ὑμᾶς ἐν Κυρίῳ εὔχομαι, ἀγαπητοὶ καὶ ποθεινότατοι υἱοί, Athanasius 26 1168 B. Cf. also Athanasius 26 1165 C, 1168 C, 1169 A, 1180 A; Basil CXCVII 288 E; Gregory of Nazianzus XLI 85 B, XLIII 89 B, CLXX 280 B, CCXI 348 C, CCXXI 361 A. Bishops also address it to deacons: διὰ τοῦ υἱοῦ ἡμῶν Ποσειδωνίου τοῦ διακόνου ἀποσταλέντα . . . γράμματα, Celestine 89 B; cf. also Basil XC 181 C, CCLXV 409 A. Bishops also make use of the term for laymen, ὁ υἱὸς Κυνήγιος, Gregory of Nyssa XIII 3; cf. also Athanasius 26 1085 A, Basil LXXII 166 B, Gregory of Nazianzus XIII 45 B, XXI 56 C, XXII 57 A, 57 C, XXIII 57 C, et passim.

CHAPTER IV

OTHER TITLES

Many titles have special uses which cannot be included in any of the foregoing chapters; they are titles for women, titles of humility, titles for the deceased, titles continued from classical usage, epithets, and finally unclassified titles.

TITLES FOR WOMEN [1]

The following titles were used in addressing women:

δέσποινα: n., *Lady.*

Δέσποινα is a title of great respect given to women of high station. So used, it occurs chiefly in the letters of St. John Chrysostom, only two examples being found elsewhere.

It is addressed to laywomen as follows: to the sisters of the emperor, ἐπιφέρεται τοίνυν τοὺς τόμους, ὥστε προσενεχθῆναι καὶ ταῖς εὐλαβεστάταις δεσποίναις καὶ τῷ φιλοχρίστῳ καὶ εὐσεβεστάτῳ δεσπότῃ, Cyril of Alexandria LXX 341 B; to Hypatia, δέσποινα μακαρία, Synesius X 1348 A; to women of rank, δέσποινά μου τιμωτάτη καὶ εὐγενεστάτη, Chrysostom CLXVIII 709 and also CCIX 728, CCXXXVIII [2] 744.

The title is given to deaconesses who were also noblewomen: ἐρρωμένη καὶ εὐθυμουμένη διατελοίης, δέσποινά μου αἰδεσιμωτάτη καὶ θεοφιλεστάτη, Chrysostom I 555; δέσποινά μου τιμωτάτη καὶ κοσμιωτάτη, Chrysostom CXCI 718; cf. also III 573, V 597, VIII 608, IX 608, XI 609, CIII 663.

κοσμιότης: n., *Decorum.*

Κοσμιότης is used especially as a title of address for women, both those of the laity and those connected with the service of the Church. We find it less frequently for laymen, and only

---

[1] For titles addressed rarely or not exclusively to women, cf. Index under *women.*

[2] Letter CCXXXVIII belongs to Constantius.

occasionally for bishops in the letters of St. Basil. The examples of its use are numerous in Basil and John Chrysostom; a single occurrence is found in Gregory of Nazianzus and in Firmus, and the title is found in no other author.

Laywomen are addressed with κοσμιότης as follows: ἔμελλον ἀποσιωπᾶν πρὸς τὴν κοσμιότητά σου, λογιζόμενος ὅτι . . . , Basil VI 78 D; γράφω μὲν ὀλιγάκις τῇ κοσμιότητί σου, Chrysostom CXVII 672. Cf. also Basil CCXCVI 434 B; Chrysostom XXXII 628, XXXIX 632, CXVII 673, CXX 675, CLXVIII 709, CXCII 719.

In the following passages, the title is given to deaconesses: ἐγὼ καὶ Σαμοσάτοις ἐπιστὰς προσεδόκησα συντεύξεσθαι τῇ κοσμιότητι ὑμῶν, Basil CV 199 C; ταῦτα ἐπιστέλλω πρὸς τὴν σὴν κοσμιότητα, Chrysostom VI 598. Cf. also Chrysostom VI 599, XI 609, CIII 663. Basil addresses it to the canoness, Theodora, CLXXIII 261 A.

The examples of its application to laymen are as follows: ἐδεξάμην τὰ γράμματα τῆς κοσμιότητος ὑμῶν, καὶ εὐχαρίστησα τῷ παναγίῳ Θεῷ, Basil CCXXVIII 351 C; ὅτι μὲν γὰρ καὶ παραγενέσθαι ἐνταῦθα οὐκ ἂν ὠκνήσατε, εἰ μὴ τὰ εἰρημένα κωλύματα παρὰ τῆς κοσμιότητος ὑμῶν ἦν, οὐδὲν ἀμφιβάλλω, Chrysostom CCXXIV 735. Cf. also Basil LXXXIII 176 D, CXLVIII 238 A, CL 239 E, CLIII 243 A, CLXXVIII 264 B, CLXXX 265 B.

Basil gives the title to bishops as follows: φοβοῦμαι δὲ περὶ τῆς σῆς κοσμιότητος, μήπου σοὶ ἐμπόδιον γένηται ἡ . . . λύπη, CCVI 309 A; cf. also CXXI 212 D, CCLIV 389 E, CCLXVI 412 E.

In Basil CLIX 247 D, the title is addressed to Eupaterius and his daughter; in Gregory of Nazianzus CCXXXVIII 381 A, to a community of monks and nuns.

In the following instances, the addressee is unidentified: Basil XXXVII 115 A, CCLXXXV 425 C, CCCXVIII 446 A; Chrysostom CLXXV 712; Firmus XXV 1500 B.

κοσμιώτατος: adj., *most decorous.*

The title κοσμιώτατος is applied only to women. It is found in the letters of Basil, Gregory of Nazianzus, Gregory of Nyssa, John Chrysostom, and Firmus.

The examples are as follows: τοῦτο καὶ νῦν ἡμῖν χάρισαι διὰ τῆς κοσμιωτάτης ἀνεψιᾶς ἡμῶν, Gregory of Nazianzus CLXXXVI 305 B;

τῇ κοσμιωτάτῃ καὶ σεμνοτάτῃ θυγατρὶ Βασιλίσσῃ Γρηγόριος ἐν Κυρίῳ χαίρειν, Nyssa III 1; καὶ τῷ φαρμάκῳ τῷ ἀπεσταλμένῳ παρὰ τῆς κυρίας μου τῆς κοσμιωτάτης Συγκλητίου, Chrysostom IV 590. Cf. also Basil CLIV 243 E, CCXCII 431 A, CCCXV 445 A, CCCXXII 448 B, CCCXXV 449 D; Gregory of Nazianzus CCVII 344 A, CCVIII 345 A; Gregory of Nyssa III 1; Chrysostom XVIII 623, XXXIII 629, XXXIX 631, XLIII 633, LVII 640, LXXI 647, XCVIII 660, XCIX 661, CXCI 718; Firmus IV 1485 A.

κυρία: n., *Madam*, *Lady*.

Κυρία is generally addressed to women of high rank and is less formal and deferential than δέσποινα. Gregory of Nazianzus uses it for members of his family.[3]

There are two instances of its occurrence in the Epistles of the New Testament: i. e., ὁ πρεσβύτερος ἐκλεκτῇ κυρίᾳ καὶ τοῖς τέκνοις αὐτῆς, οὓς ἐγὼ ἀγαπῶ ἐν ἀληθείᾳ, II John 1; καὶ νῦν ἐρωτῶ σε, κυρία, οὐχ ὡς ἐντολὴν γράφων σοι καινὴν ἀλλὰ ἣν εἴχαμεν ἀπ᾿ ἀρχῆς, ἵνα ἀγαπῶμεν ἀλλήλους, II John 5.

The other passages in which the title occurs are as follows: to deaconesses, ἀπήντησε δὲ καὶ ἡ κυρία μου Σαβινιανὴ ἡ διάκονος Chrysostom XIII 611 and XIV 617; for laywomen, καὶ τοῦτο οἶσθα καὶ αὐτή, κυρία μου κοσμιωτάτη καὶ εὐλαβεστάτη, Chrysostom XXXIII 629; κυρία μου κοσμιωτάτη καὶ εὐγενεστάτη, Chrysostom XCIX 661; cf. also Chrysostom IV 590, VIII 607, XII 610, XVIII 623, XXXIX 631, XLIII 633, XLIV 634, LVII 640, LXXI 647, XCVIII 660, CLXXVIII 713. Gregory of Nazianzus addresses it to his mother: τὴν δὲ κυρίαν τὴν μητέρα, VII 33 B; προσεδρεύομεν γὰρ τῇ κυρίᾳ τῇ μητρί, LX 120 B. Cf. also Gregory of Nazianzus CCX 348 A, to his niece.

TITLES OF HUMILITY

Titles of humility are those which an author uses in referring to himself in order to avoid the use of the first person and to express the low esteem in which he wishes to be held.

βραχύτης: n., *Unworthiness*.

Βραχύτης as a title of humility is found in the letters of Chry-

---

[3] Cf. the use of κύριος corresponding to this, p. 66.

sostom, the Cappadocians, and a few minor writers.   It appears in non-literary records as the equivalent of the first person.[4]

The examples are as follows: τοῦ μακαρίου Εὐφρασίου τοῦ ἐπισκόπου διὰ πάσης γνησιότητος ἑαυτῷ τε καὶ ὑμῖν οἷον σειραῖς τισι τῇ ἀγάπῃ τὴν βραχύτητα ἡμῶν συνδήσαντος, Nyssa XVII 2; καὶ οἶδα μὲν ὅτι σοι σπουδή, δέσποτά μου θαυμασιώτατε, καὶ ἐπιθυμία διὰ τῆς ἡμετέρας βραχύτητος τῶν ἀπορρήτων τούτων καταξιωθῆναι ἀγαθῶν, καὶ ἡμῖν δέ, ὡς αὐτὸς οἶσθα, τοῦτο περισπούδαστον, Chrysostom CXXXII 691; ὃς καὶ τὰ γράμματα τῆς ἐμῆς βραχύτητος ἐπιδίδωσι τῇ σῇ ἁγιωσύνῃ, Alypius 148 C; cf. also Basil VIII [5] 80 E, Gregory of Nazianzus CCII 332 B, Amphilochius 96 A.

εὐτέλεια: n., *Unworthiness.*

This title of humility appears only in Gregory of Nazianzus, Nilus, and Theodoret.   Preisigke records its use in non-literary material.

The examples are as follows: ... ἢ δεινότατα ἂν πάθοι μόνος ἀνθρώπων, μὴ τυγχάνων τῆς τῶν καιρῶν φιλανθρωπίας καὶ τῆς δεδομένης τοῖς ἱερατικοῖς παρὰ τῶν βασιλέων τιμῆς, ἀλλ' ὑβριζόμενος καὶ ζημιούμενος ἴσως διὰ τὴν ἡμετέραν εὐτέλειαν, Gregory of Nazianzus IX 36 C; φανερὸν τῇ ἐμῇ εὐτελείᾳ κατέστησε τὸν δόλιον καὶ πολύσπιλον δαίμονα, Nilus II 167, 280 C; Ὑπάτιον καὶ Ἀβράμιον ... δυναμένους δὲ καὶ διὰ τῆς γλώττης ἀκριβῶς ὑμᾶς διδάξαι τὰ κατὰ τὴν ὑμετέραν εὐτέλειαν, Theodoret CXVI 1325 C; τὰς εὐχαριστηρίους φωνὰς ὑπὲρ τῆς ἐμῆς εὐτελείας τῷ φιλοχρίστῳ προσενεγκεῖν βασιλεῖ, Theodoret CXXXVIII 1360 D.

εὐτελέστατος: adj., *most unworthy.*

This title of humility occurs but once in a letter of doubtful authenticity: ἐκκλησίαν ἐνυβρίζειν, μηνύσει χρησάμενος πρός με τὸν εὐτελέστατον, Basil XLI 124 B.

μετριότης: n., *Mediocrity.*

Μετριότης as a title of humility is very rare.   We have found but two examples: διόπερ συγγνώμην ἀπονέμων τῇ τε μετριότητί μου, Origen

---

[4] Preisigke s. v.

[5] This letter is probably not Basil's, and seems to belong to Evagrius of Pontus; cf. Deferrari, Vol. II, Introduction, p. 6.

49 A; τά τε νῦν γράμματα τῆς ἡμετέρας μετριότητος, a letter of bishops quoted in Athanasius 26 792 C.

οὐδένεια (written also οὐθένεια) : n., *Nothingness*.

St. John Chrysostom seems to employ οὐδένεια as a title of humility. It occurs as follows: καὶ γὰρ οἶμαί σε ἀλγεῖν οὐ διὰ ταῦτα μόνον, ἀλλὰ καὶ διὰ τὸ κεχωρίσθαι τῆς οὐδενείας τῆς ἡμετέρας, II 568 ; ἡ μὲν ὑπερβολὴ τῶν ἐγκωμίων τῶν τοῖς γράμμασιν ἐγκειμένων τῆς σῆς τιμιότητος σφόδρα ἡμῶν ὑπερβαίνει τὴν οὐθένειαν.[6]

σμικρότης : n., *Unimportance*.

In two instances σμικρότης appears to be used as a title of humility: ἀλλ᾽ οὐδέν μοι τοῦτο μέλει, κἂν καταφρονῆτε, κἂν ὑπερορᾶτε τῆς ἡμετέρας σμικρότητος, letter of Constantius in Chrysostom CCXXXIX 745 ; ἐπανελθὼν δὲ πρώην ἀπὸ τῆς ὑμετέρας ὁ θεοσεβέστατος πρεσβύτερος Εὐσέβιος, ἀπήγγειλε συνουσίαν ὑμῖν τινα γεγενῆσθαι, καὶ μεταξὺ λόγου τινὸς καὶ τὴν περὶ ἡμῶν κινηθῆναι καὶ τὴν σὴν εὐσέβειαν εὐφήμως τῆς ἐμῆς μνησθῆναι σμικρότητος, Theodoret LXII 1233 B.

ταπείνωσις : n., *Humility*.

Examples of ταπείνωσις as a title of humility are found in Gregory of Nazianzus, John Chrysostom, and Theodoret, but most frequently in Basil.

The passages in which it occurs are as follows: ἤγαγεν εἰς ἔργον ὁ Κύριος τοῦ λαοῦ αὐτοῦ τὰ αἰτήματα, καὶ ἔδωκεν αὐτῷ διὰ τῆς ἡμετέρας ταπεινώσεως ποιμένα ἄξιον μὲν τοῦ ὀνόματος, Basil CIII 198 B ; σὺ δέ, παρακαλῶ, ὑπερεύχου τῆς ταπεινώσεως ἡμῶν, Gregory of Nazianzus LXV 129 A ; καὶ εὔχεσθαι μετὰ πολλῆς ἐκτενείας ὑπὲρ τῆς ταπεινώσεως τῆς ἡμετέρας, Chrysostom XXIII 625 ; δεξάσθω τοίνυν ἡ θεοσέβειά σου τῆς ἐμῆς ταπεινώσεως τὴν παράκλησιν, Theodoret XVII 1196 C. Cf. also Basil VIII [7] 89 A, LX 155 B, CCXIII 320 A, CCXXIV 343 D, CCLVI 390 E, CCLXVII 414 A, CCXC 429 A ; Chrysostom XCII 656, XCIII 657.

[6] Vaticanus: οὐδένιαν, (Migne Edition).
[7] Letter VIII is probably not Basil's; cf. p. 79, footnote 5.

Titles for the Deceased

There are a few titles which are used in referring to deceased persons.

μακάριος: adj., *blessed;* as a substantive, *blessed one* or *my dear sir.*

The adjective μακάριος is used most frequently in referring to deceased persons, to saints of the Old and New Testaments, and to martyrs. Examples of its being addressed to the living are not common. The substantival form, ὦ μακάριε, is classical.[8] Of the authors studied, only Isidorus and the pagan Libanius make use of it. The adjectival form is used by all of the important authors except Nilus, and by many of the minor ones.

The examples of the use of μακάριος applied to deceased persons are numerous. It is used for saints as follows: for saints of the Old Testament, Ἰουδὶθ ἡ μακαρία, I Clement of Rome LV 4; τοῦ μακαρίου Δανιήλ, Athanasius 25 617 B; ὁ μακάριος Ἰώβ, Chrysostom III 579; for saints of the New Testament, τὴν ἐπιστολὴν τοῦ μακαρίου Παύλου τοῦ ἀποστόλου, I Clement of Rome XLVII 1; τῇ σοφίᾳ τοῦ μακαρίου καὶ ἐνδόξου Παύλου, Polycarp III 2; τὸν μακάριον Παύλον, Chrysostom II 569; μακαρίῳ Τίτῳ, Theodoret CXLVI 1404 C; for fathers, οἱ μακάριοι Πάτερες, Athanasius 25 665 C; ἁγίων καὶ μακαρίων Πατέρων, Theodoret LXXVII 1252 A; μακαρίων Πατέρων, Gennadius 1616 B; for martyrs, ὁ μακάριος Ἰγνάτιος, Athanasius 26 777 A; τοῦ μακαρίου μάρτυρος Εὐψυχίου, Basil CXLII 235 A.

The title is used with reference to deceased bishops as follows: ὑπομονήν, ἣν καὶ εἴδατε κατ' ὀφθαλμοὺς οὐ μόνον ἐν τοῖς μακαρίοις Ἰγνατίῳ καὶ Ζωσίμῳ καὶ Ῥούφῳ ἀλλὰ καὶ ἐν ἄλλοις, Polycarp IX 1; διελέγετο ὁ μακάριος Πολύκαρκος, Irenaeus 1228 A; ... ἀπὸ τοῦ μεγάλου προστάτου τῆς ἐκκλησίας ὑμῶν Γρηγορίου μέχρι τοῦ μακαρίου τοῦτο, Basil XXVIII 108 C; ἀπέστειλα τῆς τε τοῦ μακαρίου Ἀκακίου ἐπιστολῆς, Theodoret CXII 1312 B. Cf. also Irenaeus 1228 B, 1229 B; Athanasius 25 268 B, 557 A; Basil CCCXX 446 E; Gregory of Nazianzus XLII 88 A, CII 196 B; Gregory of Nyssa XVII 2; Synesius LXVII 1413 C; Cyril of Alexandria X 65 D, XIV 97 B, XXXIX 180 C, 181 B, XLIV 225 C, 228 C, LXIX 340 B; Alypius 148 A; John of

---

[8] Liddell and Scott s. v.

Antioch I 1453 B; Acacius 100 D; Theodoret LXXXIII 1272 C, 1273 A, LXXXVI 1277 D, CX 1305 C, CXII 1312 A, 1312 B, 1312 C, CLXX 1481 A. It is found occasionally for other ecclesiastics: to a deacon, τοῦ μακαρίου διακόνου Θεοφράστου δεξαμένου μὲν τὰ γράμματα ἡμῶν ἐπί τινα περιοδείαν ἀναγκαίως ἀποδημούντων, Basil XCV 189 A and also 189 C; to monks ἤκουσα περὶ τῆς κοιμήσεως τοῦ μακαρίου Θεοδώρου, Athanasius 26 977 D; cf. also Gregory of Nazianzus CCXXXVIII 380 C, 381 A. In the following passages, μακάριος refers to deceased relatives: τὴν μακαρίαν σου θειὰν τὴν ἀληθῶς Εὐτρόπιον, Athanasius 25 604 B; μακαρίας μητρός μου, Basil CCXXIII 338 D; ἐντρυφῶ γὰρ καὶ τῇ μνήμῃ τῆς μακαρίας, Gregory of Nazianzus CXCVII 324 A; cf. also Basil CCIV 306 B, CCC 436 A, CCCI 437 D; Gregory of Nazianzus CXCVII 321 A; Chrysostom LXXI 647, CXCII 719, CXCVII 721. For deceased persons, cf. also Athanasius 25 608 A; Basil CXXXVIII 230 A, CCXXV 345 B, CCXXXVII 366 A, CCXLIV 378 D; Gregory of Nyssa XVII 2; Theodoret CX 1305 A.

The examples of the use of μακάριος for the living are rather infrequent. They are not found after Athanasius except in the following instance in which Synesius addresses the title to Hypatia, the pagan philosopher: δέσποινα μακαρία, X 1348 A. The passages are as follows: to bishops, μακαρίῳ πάπᾳ καὶ ἐπισκόπῳ ἡμῶν ᾿Αλεξάνδρῳ οἱ πρεσβύτεροι καὶ οἱ διάκονοι ἐν Κυρίῳ χαίρειν, Arius 708 C; μακάριε πάπα, addressed to Athanasius in 26 708 C; cf. also Arius 708 C, 709 B; Athanasius 25 364 C, 372 B, 381 A, 408 B, and 26 708 C, 709 A; to a priest, τὰ γράμματα ἀπέστειλα διὰ Κλήμεντος τοῦ μακαρίου πρεσβυτέρου, Alexander of Jerusalem quoted in Eusebius H. E. VI 11, 6; to a church, . . . τῇ μακαρίᾳ ᾿Αντιοχέων ᾿Εκκλησίᾳ ἐν κυρίῳ χαίρειν, Alexander of Jerusalem quoted in Eusebius H. E. 11, 5; for the emperor, ὦ μακάριε καὶ θεοφιλέστατε Αὔγουστε, Athanasius 25 641 A.

We have noted that the classical form of address, ὦ μακάριε, occurs only in the letters of Isidorus and the pagan Libanius; for example, οὐ χρή, μακάριε, πάντα ἐπιέναι ἀναισχύντοις καὶ ἀκρατέσι τοῖς ὀφθαλμοῖς, Isidorus III 199, 881 D; ταῦτ᾿ οὖν ἅπαντα, ὦ μακάριε, . . . Isidorus III 154, 848 A; ἀλλ᾿, ὦ μακάριε, ἔασον τὴν ἀγέλην τῶν χηνῶν . . . Libanius ₍ανοζ̅ʹ 4. Cf. also Isidorus IV 129, 1205 D, 145, 1225 C;

224, 1317 A; V 20, 1336 C; 78, 1372 D; 215, 1460 C; 222, 1465 C; 321, 1521 C; Libanius ρ϶ϛ' 2, τπβ' 3, χνϛ' 2.

The following examples are uncertain but are probably addressed to deceased persons: Alexander of Jerusalem quoted in Eusebius H. E. VI 19, 18 and VI 14, 9; Basil LXVII 160 E; Chrysostom XII 609; Cyril of Alexandria LXXVI 357 A; Atticus 349 C; Isidorus I 173, 296 B; II 151, 604 C; III 304, 973 D; 331, 989 A; V 28, 1341 A; 388, 1560 B; Theodoret XCVII 1292 B.

μακαρίτης: adj., *blessed, happily departed.*

Μακαρίτης is used always of deceased persons, apparently of those who were living within the lifetime of the writer. Preisigke records its occurrence in the same sense.

Examples of its use for the emperors are as follows: παρὰ τοῦ μακαρίτου Κωνσταντίνου τοῦ Αὐγούστου, Athanasius 25 581 A; ὁ μακαρίτης Κωνστάντιος, Julian XLVIII. Cf. also Athanasius 25 357 A, 581 A, 582 B, 601 A, 604 A, 604 D, 605 A, 605 B; Julian XV, XIX, XXI, XXIV, XXX, and letter LVII which is of doubtful authenticity but of early date.

It is referred to bishops in the following instances: ἀπέθανεν οὖν ὁ συλλειτουργὸς ἡμῶν ὁ μακαρίτης Θεόδουλος, Athanasius 25 328 B; ἀπέστειλα τῆς τε τοῦ μακαρίου 'Ακακίου ἐπιστολῆς, καὶ τῆς τοῦ μακαρίου 'Ιωάννου πρὸς τὸν μακαρίτην Κύριλλον, Theodoret CXII 1312 B. Cf. also Athanasius 25 237 C, 257 B, 532 A, 357 A, 480 A, 485 A, 488 C, 564 B, 580 B, 588 B, 613 A, 688 A, 708 C; Synesius LXVII 1413 C; Theodoret CXII 1312 C.

Synesius applies μακαρίτης to persons who are unknown to us: XVIII 1353 A, XX 1353 C, XXXVI 1361 D, XLIV 1368 A, LX 1404 B, LXI 1405 A, LXVI 1408 D.

μακαριώτατος: adj., *most blessed.*

The title μακαριώτατος is generally given to deceased bishops. There are, however, rare instances of its use for living bishops. Μακαριώτατος is found in all the important authors of the fourth and fifth centuries except John Chrysostom, Cyril of Alexandria, and Isidorus.

The examples for deceased bishops are as follows: ἐγὼ δέ, εἶπέ μοι, τὸν μακαριώτατον Διάνιον ἀνεθεμάτισα, Basil LI 143 D; τὴν μνήμην

4

τοῦ μακαριωτάτου Πέτρου παρὰ Σεβαστηνοῖς πρώτως ἀγομένην ἐπιτελέσας, Gregory of Nyssa I 5; ἐπιστολήν, τήν τε τοῦ μακαριωτάτου καὶ ἐν ἁγίοις Ἀθανασίου, ἣν πρὸς τὸν μακάριον Ἐπίκτητον ἔγραψεν, Theodoret 1277 D. Cf. also Basil LXX 164 B, CXXXIII 225 D, CLIV 243 D, CXCVII 288 B, CCIV 306 B, 306 D, CCXIV 521 C, CCLVIII 394 B, CCLXIII 406 A, 406 C; Theodoret LXXXI 1261 A, CX 1305 C, CXIII 1316 C. Basil addresses it once to the martyr Eutyches, CC 298 D.

It is addressed to living bishops in a few passages: μακαριώτατε πάπα, addressed to Athanasius 25 373 A; πρὸς τὴν μακαριωτάτην σου κεφαλήν, Synesius LXVII 1413 B; cf. also Athanasius 25 353 B.

The following examples are uncertain: Athanasius 26 820 C; Gregory of Nazianzus CCXXII 361 C; Synesius LXXVI 1441 B; Nilus II 265, 336 B; III 31, 385 D.

TITLES CONTINUED FROM CLASSICAL USAGE

Many titles in the letters of this period are also found in classical Greek literature, usually in Plato and Aristophanes. The titles appear to be a device to give the desired literary finish to letters.

ἀγαθός: substantive *good sir* or *good friend*.

The vocative ὦ ἀγαθέ or the shortened form ὦ 'γαθέ occur very rarely as a term of address among Christian writers. Isidorus and Synesius are the only authors who employ it. Its use as a title goes back, however, to Plato and the philosophical writers. The pagan Libanus uses it rather frequently.

The examples are as follows: ἐπεὶ δὲ διαφέρει σοι τἀμὰ εἰδέναι, φιλοσοφοῦμεν, ὦ 'γαθέ, τὴν ἐρημίαν ἀγαθὴν ἔχοντες συνεργόν, ἄνθρωπον δὲ οὐδένα, Synesius C 1469 C; οὐ πλουτοῦμεν, ὦ 'γαθέ, ἀλλὰ τὰ παρόντα ἀρκεῖ καὶ Πυλαιμένει κἀμοί, Synesius CXXXIII 1521 B; ἴσθι, ὦ ἀγαθέ, ὅτι . . . Isidorus V 221, 1464 C; εἰ μόλις, ὦ ἀγαθέ, . . . Isidorus V 323, 1521 D; ἀλλ', ὠγαθέ, καὶ θέλε θαρρεῖν καὶ ἐπιστέλλειν, Libanius λβ' 1; ἀλλ', ὦ 'γαθέ, μὴ διάγραφε τὰς Χάριτας, Libanius σκα' 4; cf. also Libanius τμη' 8, τϚα' 2, υλβ' 2, χκα' 2, χκδ' 2, ͵ασλε' 4, ͵ασμγ' 3, ͵ασξζ' 1, ͵ατϚε' 3, ͵αυκϚ' 5, ͵αυνθ' 4. Cf. also his use of the expression ὁ πάντα ἀγαθός; Εὐθήριος ὁ πάντα ἀγαθός, ρζ' 1; ὁ πάντα ἀγαθὸς ἔγραψε βασιλεύς, υλδ' 2.

The irregular superlative ἀγαθώτατος occurs once in a letter of Julian to the sophist Priscus: ἀγαθώτατε, πότε σε ἴδω καὶ περιλά-βωμαι, V.

ἄνθρωπε: n., *man, sir.*

The vocative ἄνθρωπε is found in address as early as Herodotus. It occurs frequently in Plato, but rarely in the dramatists. Since ἄνθρωπε was a term of address for slaves, it was often used in a contemptuous sense. This idea of disdain is prevalent in all the examples of its occurrence in Christian literature.

In the Epistles of the New Testament, ἄνθρωπε occurs in passages of disdainful reproach: λογίζῃ δὲ τοῦτο, ὦ ἄνθρωπε ὁ κρίνων τοὺς τὰ τοιαῦτα πράσσοντας καὶ ποιῶν αὐτά, ὅτι σὺ ἐκφεύξῃ τὸ κρίμα τοῦ Θεοῦ, Rom. II 3; ὦ ἄνθρωπε, μενοῦνγε σὺ τίς εἶ ὁ ἀνταποκρινόμενος τῷ Θεῷ, Rom. IX 20. Cf. also Rom. II 1, II James 20.

We find no examples in early Christian epistles. Among the later Christian writers, ἄνθρωπε keeps its derogatory sense, and is addressed only to those who are being rebuked or exhorted. Nilus alone uses it commonly. It occurs rarely in Basil, once in Isidorus, and once in the letters of Dionysius Areopagitus. The precise sense varies from angry reproach, as in Basil CLX 251 C, μὴ ποιήσῃς, ὦ ἄνθρωπε, τὴν θείαν μητρυιὰν τῶν νηπίων; to pity, τί μοχθεῖς, ἄνθρωπε, καὶ κάμνεις ἀπέραντα, Nilus II 179, 292 C; and exhortation, γρηγόρησον, ἄνθρωπε, Nilus IV 18, 560 A. The remaining examples are as follows: Basil VIII [9] 87 A, CCXXIII 339 C, Nilus I 6, 85 A; 13, 88 B; 50, 105 A; 79, 117 A; 319, 197 B; II 45, 217 A; 149, 269 B; 273, 337 D; 330, 361 C; III 112, 436 B; 141, 448 D; 243, 497 B and 500 C; 296, 529 D; IV 12, 556 A; 39, 568 D; Isidorus II 100, 544 C; Dionysius Areopagitus VIII 1089 B.

βέλτιστος: adj., *my good*; as a substantive, *my good friend.*

Βέλτιστε is addressed to all classes of persons and indicates a friendly relation between the writer and addressee. It is very common as a term of familiar address in Plato.[10] Isidorus alone among

---

[9] This letter probably belongs not to Basil but to Evagrius of Pontus; cf. p. 79, footnote 5.

[10] Liddell and Scott s. v.

the Christian writers of letters employs it commonly. It appears rarely in Cyril of Alexandria, Gregory of Nazianzus, Nilus, and Procopius. Libanius makes frequent use of it.

The passages in which it occurs are as follows: σὺ μὲν διὰ τοῦτο ἀτιμάζεις, ὦ βέλιστε, τὸν ἐμὸν νοῦν, Gregory of Nazianzus CI 185 C; ἐγώ σοι λέγω, ὅτι οὐκ ἀπογνωστέον, ὦ βέλτιστε, Nilus III 274, 520 C; φεύγετε ὦ βέλτιστοι, τὴν κακίαν, Isidorus V 11, 1332 A; εἶτα τίς ὁ κενώσας ἑαυτόν, ὦ βέλτιστοι, καὶ πῶς τεταπείνωται, Cyril of Alexandria L 260 D. Cf. also Isidorus I 79, 237 A; 345, 380 C; II 9, 464 D; 94, 537 D; 158, 613 A; 165, 617 C; 278, 709 A; 284, 713 B, et passim; Cyril of Alexandria I 24 C, XL 193 A; L 260 B; Procopius I 2720 B, LII 2760 A, LXXVI 2777 D.

βέλτιστος has also an adjectival use as a title of esteem: συγχαίρω τῷ βελτίστῳ Σαραπίωνι, quoted in Athanasius 25 368 A; κἂν γὰρ κεκοίμηται ὁ βέλτιστος υἱός σου Νικάρετος, Nilus II 170, 285 C; τὰς ἐπιστολὰς ἄσμενος διὰ τοῦ βελτίστου Μυγδονίου, Julian XXXIII; τὸν δὲ βέλτιστον Μέγαν, Procopius XXIII 2740 A.

γενναῖος: adj., *noble;* as a substantive, *noble friend, noble sir.*

The substantive γενναῖε is a common form of address in Plato. There is but one example of its use among Christian authors: ἀλλ' ἀνδριστέον, ὦ γενναῖε, γενναῖος γὰρ εἴης, Synesius XLIV 1369 C to a certain John. We find it in the letters of the pagan Libanius: ἔπραξας, ὦ γενναῖε, σοφίᾳ χρησάμενος ὑπὲρ τῆς ἀληθείας, letter χνη′ 1; cf. also Ϛζ′ 6, ση′ 4, σιε′ 4, τπθ′ 3, ωξζ′ 3, et passim; also the letter of doubtful authenticity attributed to Libanius in the Basilian corpus, μὴ σύ γε, ὦ γενναῖε, ἀλλὰ γενοῦ πρᾶος καὶ δὸς ἀπολαῦσαι τῆς παγχρύσου σου γλώττης, CCCXLI 456 E. There are several instances of its use in the letters of Julian, also of doubtful authenticity: τὸ γῆρας ἡμῖν ἐτριπλασίασας, ὦ γενναῖε, LII; ὦ γενναῖε, ποτεῖς, LXVII; also letters LXXVII, LXXVIII, LXXIX.

In its adjectival use as a title, or rather as an epithet, the following examples of γενναῖος occur in the Christian writers of letters: αἱ τῶν Ἑβραίων ἱστορίαι φασίν, ὦ γενναῖε Δημόφιλε, Dionysius Areopagitus VIII 1084 B; ἀλλ' οὗτος μὲν ὁ γενναῖος, ἀπάτῃ τὴν ἀπειλὴν κεράσας, μεταναστῆναι τῆς εὐσεβοῦς τοὺς πάντας καὶ προὐτρέπετο καὶ κατηνάγκαζε γνώμης, Peter II of Alexandria quoted in Theodoret

H. E. 22, 16; οἷα γὰρ ὑμῖν ἐνεδείξατο ὁ γενναῖος Βασίλειος, Basil CXIX
210 D; ὁ τὰ πάντα γενναῖος Ἄνθιμος, Basil CXXII 213 B. Γενναῖος
in each of these instances has an ironical sense.

The pagans use the adjective γενναῖος as a term of address with
the ordinary connotation of noble: ἀνεμνήσθην γὰρ τοῦ γενναίου καὶ
πάντα θαυμασίου πατρὸς ἡμῶν, Julian LXVIII; ἠρόμην τὸν γενναῖον
Εὐσέβιον, Libanius νηθ' 1; ὑποθέσεως δὲ οὐκ ἀπορήσεις τῶν γενναίων ἡμῖν
βασιλέων ἀεί τι καλὸν ἐργαζομένων, Libanius ϩμδ' 2; πρὸς τὸν γενναῖον
Παλλάδιον ἔγραψας, Libanius, ͵αρξθ' 7; et passim.

γλυκύτατος: adj., most sweet, most dear.

Γλυκύτατος is used as a title of affection or intimacy, addressed to
inferiors and to relatives. The non-literary records show a similar
usage.[11] It occurs as a term of address in Aristophanes. We find
an illustration of its use in the letters of Ignatius, which, though
not a title, approaches the conventional usage of the term in later
times: τῶν διακόνων, τῶν ἐμοὶ γλυκυτάτων, to the Magnesians VI, 1.

Chrysostom twice addresses a priest with γλυκύτατος: ὁ ποθεινότατος καὶ γλυκύτατος Ἰωάννης ὁ πρεσβύτερος, LV 640 and also LIII
638. It is given to children in the following passages: τὸν δεσπότην
μου τὸν τιμιώτατον καὶ εὐλαβέστατον πρεσβύτερον Ἀσυγκρίτιον, μετὰ τῶν
γλυκυτάτων αὐτοῦ παιδίων, Chrysostom CXIV 671; τὰ γλυκύτατα παιδία,
Firmus IV 1485 A; τῷ τε γὰρ γλυκυτάτῳ τῷδε τὴν παρὰ τῇ θαυμασιότητί
σου δέδωκας καταφυγήν, Firmus XXV 1500 B. Gregory of Nazianzus
uses it in addressing Nicobulus, his nephew: ὁ γλυκύτατος υἱὸς ἡμῶν
Νικόβουλος, CLXXXVIII 308 B; cf. also CLXVII 277 A, CLXXVI
288 B, CLXXXVII 308 A.

The title occurs also in Gregory of Nazianzus CCXXX 373 A,
Chrysostom CCXIX 732.

δαιμόνιε: n., good sir.

The title, δαιμόνιε, is found only in Libanius. As a term of
address, it is a classical usage, occurring especially in Homer,
Aristophanes, and Plato.[12] The examples are as follows: ἀλλὰ
τούτους γε τοὺς πένητας, ὦ δαιμόνιε, πλήρωμα μὲν εἶναι τῇ βουλῇ βούλου,

---

[11] Moulton and Milligan s. v.; Preisigke s. v.
[12] Liddell and Scott s. v.

μ´ 2; πρῶτον μὲν δὴ ταύτην, ὦ δαιμόνιε, τὴν σύγχρισιν ἀξίου διορίζειν, σνα´ 7; cf. also σοδ´ 2, τϚθ´ 3, νγ´ 2, φκη´ 4, ψοθ´ 5, ωι´ 7, ͵ατϚ´ 1.

θαυμόσιος: adj., *admirable*; as a substantive, *admirable sir* or *admirable friend.*

The term θαυμάσιε or ὦ θαυμάσιε was used in address as early as Plato. Among the authors of the fourth and fifth centuries, we have found examples of its use in the Cappadocians, Isidorus, and Theodoret. It occurs also in the letters of Julian and Libanius. It is addressed to men of all stations in life but more frequently to laymen, and generally to persons with whom the author's relations were friendly.

The examples are as follows:

To bishops: μὴ οὖν εἰς ἄλλον καιρὸν ὑπέρθῃ τὴν ἐπίσκεψιν αὐτῆς, ὦ θαυμάσιε, Basil CXLV 236 D; μηδαμῶς, ὦ θαυμάσιε, μὴ οὕτως ἔχε, Gregory of Nazianzus LXXXI 156 A. Cf. also Basil XXV 104 B, and the unauthentic letter, CCCLXIII 465 D; Gregory of Nazianzus L 104 B, LVIII 116 A; Gregory of Nyssa XXVI 2; Isidorus I 104, 253 A; 324, 369 C; 451, 429 D; II 127, 565 B; III 75, 781 C; 142, 837 D; 245, 924 A.

To a priest: ὦ θαυμάσιε, Isidorus III 271, 949 D.

To deacons: σύμβολόν ἐστιν, ὦ θαυμάσιε, Isidorus III 226, 909 A; cf. also I 373, 393 C; II 148, 604 A; V 451, 1588 C.

To a lector: περὶ ὧν μετέρχῃ ἄθλων, θαυμάσιε, πέπεισο, Isidorus I 4, 181 B.

To monks: τοῦτο, θαυμάσιε, τοῦ παράφρονος Ἀπολλιναρίου τὸ ἀτόπημα, letters to the monk Caesarius among the spuria of Chrysostom 757, and 760; cf. also Serapion 936 A.

To laymen of high station: οἷα ποιεῖς, ὦ θαυμάσιε, τὴν φίλην ἡμῖν πενίαν καὶ φιλοσοφίας τροφὸν τῆς ἐσχατιᾶς ἀπελαύνων, Basil IV 76 C; σκόπησον, ὦ θαυμάσιε, τίς ἐστι μᾶλλον ἀγρίπιστος, Gregory of Nyssa XXVII 1; ἅρπασον τοίνυν, ὦ θαυμάσιε, τὸ δῶρον, Theodoret LXXVII 1245 C. Cf. also Basil LXIII 157 B, LXXXIV 177 C, XCIV 187 C, CLXXXIII 266 B, CCXIV 322 A, also CCCXXXIX 455 D and CCCXLVIII 459 B, letters which are considered spurious; Gregory of Nazianzus XI 41 C, CXXXIV 229 B, CXLI 241 B, CXLVI 249 C, CLXVI 276 B, CLXXVI 288 A, CLXXIX

296 B, CLXXXIX 308 C, CXCIII 316 C, CXCVIII 324 C, CCI 329 A; Gregory of Nyssa XIV 8; Synesius XIX 1353 B, CLIV 1557 B; Isidorus II 179, 629 D; 237, 676 B; III 40, 760 A; 158, 853 B; 375, 1024 B; V 106, 1388 B; 277, 1497 D; Nilus II 32, 212 D.

Cf. also the following passages in which the addressee is not known: Basil CXCIV 286 B, CCLXXXIX 428 B, CCCI 437 E; Gregory of Nazianzus CXLVIII 253 A; Synesius XCII 1457 C, CXXVI 1505 C, CXXXII 1520 B, CXLVI 1544 B, CXLVIII 1549 D; Isidorus I 56, 220 A; 447, 428 D; III 317, 981 B; IV 196, 1284 C; 271, 1493 D.

The adjectival form is used occasionally as an epithet: τούτων εἶς ἐστι καὶ ὁ θαυμάσιος 'Αμαζόνιος, Gregory of Nazianzus XCIV 168 C; τὸν θαυμάσιον κόμητα πρόσειπε, Synesius CXLI 1553 C. Cf. also Gregory of Nyssa XI 3; Synesius IV 1341 B, XXVI 1356 D, LXXIX 1448 A, CXXX 1513 C, CXLIV 1541 A, CXXX 1515 C; Theodoret CXXIII 1333 D; Procopius XL 2749 C; Julian LXVIII; Libanius ρπθ' 1, ϱιθ' 2, ϱμγ' 1, ϱπ' 4, ‚αιε' 1, ‚ανθ' 4, ‚αρν' 2.

θαυμαστός: adj., admirable.

Θαυμαστός is used occasionally as an epithet.

In classical Greek literature, ὦ θαυμαστέ as a term of address had an ironical connotation.[13] This usage occurs in the following passages from the letters which we have examined: ὁ δὲ θαυμαστὸς Γρηγόριος, Athanasius 25 232 A; οἱ δὲ περὶ Εὐσέβιον οἱ θαυμαστοί, Athanasius 25 265 B; ἀλλὰ καὶ γράμμα τοῦ θαυμαστοῦ Βασιλείου κομίζων ἡμῖν, Basil CCCXXXVI 453 B, a letter which is considered spurious; ὁ θαυμαστὸς Ἰωάννης, μικρὸν εἰπεῖν, Synesius CX 1493 A; ὁ θαυμαστὸς Κυρήνιος κατέπτη, Isidorus I 177, 298 A.

Θαυμαστός is also used in a complimentary sense: ἐπὶ τοῦ θαυμαστοῦ Γρηγορίου, Basil CCVII 311 E; ἀπέλιπεν ἡμᾶς ὁ θαυμαστὸς 'Αλύπιος ὁ κοινὸς τῶν φίλων προστάτης, καὶ τῶν ὀρφανῶν κηδεμών, Gregory of Nazianzus CCVIII 345 A; πατρὸς δὲ ἐμοῦ καὶ διδασκάλου τοῦ θαυμαστοῦ Βασιλείου, Gregory of Nyssa XIII 4; τοῦ θαυμαστοῦ Διοσκόρου, Synesius LXVII 1424 A.

Libanius makes frequent use of it, for example: Βάσσου τοῦ

---

13 Liddell and Scott s. v.

θαυμαστοῦ, τνδ' 9; ὁ θαυμαστὸς 'Εκδίκιος, ,ατνδ' 2; also ωιη' 2, ϡν' 3, ,ασκγ' 1, et passim.

Further references for θαυμαστός are as follows: Athanasius 25 640 B; Gregory XI of Nyssa 5; Synesius XXXIII 1361 B, XLVII 1376 C, LIII 1380 D, LXVII 1432 B, LXXXII 1453 B, LXXXIII 1453 C, LXXXIV 1453 D, LXXXV 1456 A, CXXVI 1505 C; Isidorus I 226, 324 B; Procopius XXIV 2740 A, XXVIII 2741 B, LXXXIV 2784 C.

καλὸς καὶ ἀγαθός: adj., *excellent.*

The expression καλὸς καὶ ἀγαθός or καλὸς κἀγαθός seems to be used as a title corresponding to the noun καλοκἀγαθία. In classical Greek literature, the term signified an aristocrat [14] or a gentleman.[15] There are only two instances addressed to persons who are identified: to Alypius, former prefect of Cappadocia, τὴν τοῦ καλοῦ καὶ ἀγαθοῦ 'Αλυπίου ποτὲ γυναῖκα, Gregory of Nazianzus CCVII 334 A; to Sacerdos, priest, ὁ καλός τε καὶ ἀγαθὸς Σακερδὼς ὁ συμπρεσβύτερος, Gregory of Nazianzus CCXVIII 356 B. For other examples, cf. Basil CCLXXVII 421 C; Firmus XXX 1501 C; Libanius χοε' 1, ϡοθ' 1, ,αροζ' 2, ,ατξδ' 1.

λῷστος: adj., *my good;* as a substantive, *my good friend.*

As a term of address, λῷστος is found in Plato and appears again in the letters of the scholar Synesius and the sophist Procopius. The examples are rare: ὦ λῷστε Πυλαίμενες, Synesius CIII 1473 C; φιλοχρημάτως ἔχεις, ὦ λῷστε, Procopius I 2720 B; ὡς ἔοικεν, ὦ λῷστε, τῶν εἰς ἡμᾶς σκωμμάτων οὔ ποτε παύῃ, Procopius VIII 2725 D; cf. also Procopius XXXII 2745 A, XCVI 2792 B.

τέκνον: n., *Child.*

Τέκνον occurs rarely as a term of address in the letters of the period in which we are interested. In classical Greek literature, it is found as early as Homer addressed by elders to younger persons.[16] It is recorded as occurring in papyri, often with refer-

---

[14] Smyth, *Greek Grammar for Colleges*, p. 274.
[15] Liddell and Scott s. v.
[16] Liddell and Scott s. v.

ence to adults.[17] The Epistles of the New Testament have several examples of this usage in the case of disciples: τέκνον Τιμόθεε, I Tim. I 18; Τίτῳ γνησίῳ τέκνῳ, Titus I 4; μειζοτέραν τούτων οὐκ ἔχω χάριν, ἵνα ἀκούω τὰ ἐμὰ τέκνα ἐν τῇ ἀληθείᾳ περιπατοῦντα, III John 4; [18] cf. also I Tim. I 2, II Tim. I 2, II 2, I Cor. IV 7. In early Christian epistles, we find several instances of its use by Pseudo-Barnabas: ^{ɔɹɔχɔoodu} τέκνα, τί λέγει τὸ συνετέλεσεν ἐν ἐξ ἡμέραις, XV 4; cf. also VII 1, IX 7, XV 4, XXI 9.

Among later writers, Nilus alone makes use of τέκνον in direct address: to a disciple, φεῦγε ἡδονήν, ὦ τέκνον, IV 1, 548 C; ἐγὼ μέν, τέκνον, ὃ ἦ ἐν ἐμοί, πεποίηκα IV 1, 549 B; cf. also IV 1, 549 A. Chrysostom uses it in referring to his friend, the bishop Pergamius: τῷ κυρίῳ μου δὲ τῷ ποθεινοτάτῳ τέκνῳ ἡμῶν Περγαμίῳ, XI 609. Cyril of Alexandria addresses it to a priest, διὰ τοῦ τέκνου ἡμῶν Ἰννοκεντίου τοῦ πρεσβυτέρου, LXXXV 377 A.

φιλότης: n., *Beloved, Friend.*

The expression ὦ φιλότης is found as a term of address in Plato.[19] Among the Christian writers, it is used chiefly by Isidorus, only two examples occurring elsewhere.

The passages in which it occurs are as follows: γαστριμαργία κέκληται, ὦ φιλότης, ἡ περιττότης, Isidorus I 384, 400 B; ἀλλὰ μακρο- θύμει, ὦ φιλότης, Isidorus III 44, 761 A; θεώρησον, ὦ φιλότης, τῆς ἀποστολικῆς ἀγάπης τὴν φλόγα, Theodoret XXI 1200 B; οὐκ ἐμπεδοῖς τὰ ὡμολογημένα πρὸς ἡμᾶς, ὦ φιλότης, Synesius CXLII 1536 A. Cf. also Isidorus I 107, 256 A; 278, 345 C; 456, 433 A; II 111, 552 C; 126, 564 D; V 525, 1624 D.

φίλτατος: adj., *dearest*; as a substantive, *my dearest friend.*

The adjective φίλτατος is found rarely as a term of address in the Christian writers. The pagan Libanius, however, makes fre- quent use of it.[20]

---

[17] Moulton and Milligan s. v.

[18] St. John prefers the form τεκνία: καὶ νῦν, τεκνία, μένετε ἐν αὐτῷ, I John II 28; also 1 and 12.

[19] Liddell and Scott s. v.

[20] The Emperor Julian uses the superlative of the adjective φιλικός as a title: ἀδελφὲ ποθεινότατε καὶ φιλικώτατε, I; cf. also V, VII.

The examples are as follows: τῷ ὄντι γάρ, φίλτατε παίδων, μόνον περισπούδαστον καὶ ἐπαινετὸν τὸ διαρκὲς ἀγαθόν, Basil CCLXXVII 421 E; Εὐώπιον ἡ φιλτάτη, Gregory of Nazianzus CCXXXI 373 B; ὦ φίλτατε καὶ θαυμάσιε, Synesius CXXXII 1520 B; καὶ τοίνυν, ὦ φίλτατε βροτῶν, ἔφην ὡς ἀπὼν ἄγαν ἐλύπεις, Procopius XXVII 2741 A; ἀλλ', ὦ φίλτατε, λογισάμενος . . . , Libanius τοθ' 9. Cf. also Synesius CXXXII 1520 A; CXXXIII 1521 B; Isidorus V 236, 1476 B; 399, 1565 B; Libanius ξα' 1, ξγ' 2, ρν' 4, τϚθ' 8, ‚ασγ' 3.

ψυχή: n., *Soul, Self.*

The use of ψυχή as a periphrasis for *man* or *individual* is common in both classical [21] and Biblical [22] Greek. It is also found in early Christian Greek in such passages as the following: διὸ μακαρίζει μου ἡ ψυχὴ τὴν εἰς Θεὸν αὐτοῦ γνώμην, Ignatius to the Philadelphians I 2. As a term of address, ψυχή is noted for classical authors.[23] For the period in which we are interested, it is used by the following writers: Athanasius, Gregory of Nazianzus, Nilus, Chrysostom, Synesius, and Theodoret.

The title occurs in letters to bishops as follows: ὀναίμην ὑμῶν τῆς φιλοχρίστου ψυχῆς, Alexander of Alexandria I 572 A; δεόμεθά σου τῆς ἀγαθῆς ψυχῆς, Basil L [24] 142 E; πειθέσθω ἡ θεοφιλής σου ψυχή, Theodoret CXXIII 1336 A. Cf. also Chrysostom LXIV 644, CXII 669; Nestorius 56 C.

Ψυχή is used in addressing laymen in the following passages: διὸ μηδαμῶς ἀπογνῶμεν, ὦ ψυχὴ πολυαμάρτητε, καὶ ἀξία τῆς αἰωνίου κολάσεως, Nilus IV 39, 569 A; ὡς τῇ διανοίᾳ καὶ ἐπιστέλλομεν καὶ προσφθεγγόμεθα συνεχῶς, μᾶλλον δὲ διηνεκῶς, τὴν εὐγενεστάτην καὶ ἐμμελεστάτην ὑμῶν ψυχήν, καὶ ἐγκολάψαντες ὑμᾶς τῷ συνειδότι, πανταχοῦ περιφέρομεν, Chrysostom C 661; cf. also Gregory of Nazianzus XXII 57 B; Chrysostom CCIV 726; Nilus II 320, 356 C.

It occurs also in addressing women: ἀρκεῖ δὲ καὶ μόνος ὁ θεο-

---

[21] Liddell and Scott s. v.

[22] Thayer s. v.; Cremer s. v.

[23] Liddell and Scott: cf. article on ψυχή, II, 2.

[24] Wittig ascribes this letter to St. John Chrysostom. The passage quoted contains the only example of this use of ψυχή in the letters of St. Basil. St. John Chrysostom, moreover, uses it not infrequently.

φιλέστατος καὶ ὁσιώτατος ἐπίσκοπος, πᾶσαν τῇ πιστοτάτῃ σου ψυχῇ παραψυχὴν πραγματεύσασθαι, Theodoret XIV 1189 D ; cf. also Chrysostom II 556, III 575, XIV 612.

Ψυχή is used as a term of address in the following instances : to Pope Innocent, παρακαλῶ τὴν ἄγρυπνον ὑμῶν ψυχήν, Chrysostom 536 ; to the emperor, ἐνθυμούμενος τὴν φιλανθρωπίαν καὶ τὴν φιλόχριστον αὐτοῦ ψυχήν, Athanasius 25 605 C ; to archimandrites, τὰ γράμματα τῆς ἱερᾶς σου ψυχῆς, Theodoret L 1225 D, and also CXXVIII 1340 D. Cf. also Synesius CXLVIII 1549 C, Chrysostom CXXIV 678.

There are several passages in which the use of ψυχή as a title is doubtful : Chrysostom II 558, 571, VII 602, XVII 621, XCVI 660, CXV 671 ; Synesius X 1348 B, XXXVIII 1364 A, LXVII 1426 A.

EPITHETS

Certain adjectives seem to be in common use as epithets rather than as conventional titles. They are as follows :

γνήσιος : adj., sincere, true.

The use of γνήσιος as a title is doubtful. The few examples indicate rather its use as an epithet. Moulton and Milligan observe that γνήσιος " becomes an epithet of affectionate appreciation."

There are three illustrations in the Epistles of the New Testament : ναὶ ἐρωτῶ καὶ σέ, γνήσιε σύνζυγε, Philip. IV 3 ; Τιμοθέῳ γνησίῳ τέκνῳ ἐν πίστει, I Tim. I 2 ; Τίτῳ γνησίῳ τέκνῳ, Titus I 4.

The later examples are as follows : ἔπειτα κἀκεῖνο διενοούμην μετὰ τῶν ἐνταῦθα γνησίων ἀδελφῶν, καὶ καθ' ἑαυτοὺς ἠσχάλλομεν, Athanasius 26 684 B ; ὦ γνήσιε ἀδελφέ, letter XLII 125 B of the Basilian corpus which has been attributed to St. Nilus ; ἀλλ' ὦ τιμιώτατον καὶ γνήσιον θρέμμα τῆς Ἐκκλησίας, βεβαίωσον καὶ ἐμοὶ τὰς ἐλπίδας, Basil LXXIII 167 E ; cf. also Athanasius 26 789 C, Basil CCCXX 447 B.

καλός : adj., good.

Καλός appears to be used as an epithet rather than as a formal title. It was so used in Attic.[25] As a term of address, it is rather colorless and is used of all classes of persons.

The examples are as follows : σὺ τὸν καλὸν ἡμῶν πάπαν Ἀπολλινάριον

---

[25] Liddell and Scott s. v.

ἄσπασαι, Origen 85 D ; ἐρεῖ δέ σοι ὁ καλὸς Πατρίκιος, Chrysostom XIV 612 ; τοῦ καλοῦ Δωροθέου τοῦ ἐπισκόπου, Cyril of Alexandria VIII 60 B ; ταῦτα, ὦ καλὲ Διονύσιε, θείων ἀμοιβαὶ πραγμάτων, Pseudo-Dionysius the Areopagite, VII 1081 C. Cf. also Basil CCXXXIX 368 C; Gregory of Nazianzus XCVII 169 C, CLXXVII 289 A, CLXXXIX 308 C, CXC 309 A, CCXXII 361 C; Chrysostom XIV 615, LXI 642 ; Procopius of Gaza III 2721 B, XVII 2733 B, XXX 2744 A, XLIX 2757 A, LXI 2768 B, LXIV 2769 D, LXXXIII 2784 B; Pseudo-Dionysius IX 1104 B.

The pagans make frequent use of it : τοῦ καλοῦ Συμμάχου, Julian L, and also XIV, LXIX ; ὦ καλὲ Λεόντιε, Libanius πη' 2 ; οἷόν με ἠδίκησας, ὦ καλὲ Μένανδρε, Libanius χοβ' 1 ; Ῥουφῖνος δὲ ὁ καλὸς τὸν κολοφῶνα ἐπέθηκε, Libanius ψλε' 4 ; also μγ' 2, ρνη' 3, ‚ατξη' 4, ‚ατπη' 2, ‚αυκς' 1, ‚αφα' 1, et passim.

μέγας: adj., great.

The adjective μέγας is fairly common as an epithet. The instances of its occurrence are as follows :

To the emperor : ὅθεν μοι δοκεῖ καὶ βασιλεὺς ὁ μέγας, Basil XCIV 188 A ; θεοπροβλήτου ἡμῶν μεγάλου βασίλεως, Isidorus IV 144, 1225 A.

To officials : ἐν καὶ τοῦτο τῆς ἀγαθῆς ἀρχῆς τοῦ μεγάλου ἀπηλαύσαμεν Θηρασίου, Basil LXXVII 172 A ; τοὺς μεγάλους ἄρχοντας, Theodoret LXXIX 1256 D; cf. also Gregory of Nazianzus XXXVIII 80 A, CCVII 344 B; Synesius XLIX 1377 A, LXXIX 1448 B; Theodoret CXII 1312 A.

To bishops : τοῦ μεγαλοῦ καὶ ἀληθινοῦ ἐπισκόπου, Basil L 143 A ; ἀεὶ προτιμήσας ἐμαυτοῦ τὸν μέγαν Βασίλειον, Gregory of Nazianzus LIII 109 A ; cf. also Athanasius 25 556 C, 557 A, 649 B, 656 C; Gregory of Nazianzus XXV 61 A, LVIII 116 A; John of Antioch I 1453 A. It is applied to eminent bishops who were deceased : τοῦ μεγάλου Ἀχιλλᾶ, Athanasius 25 592 B ; ἐπὶ τοῦ μεγάλου Γρηγορίου, Basil CCVII 311 D ; τὰ τοῦ μεγάλου Βασιλείου συγγράμματα, Theodoret CXLV 1384 C; cf. also Theodoret CXII 1309 B, CXLVI 1404 B.

Of saints and martyrs : καὶ τῶν μεγάλων καὶ μακαρίων ἀποστόλων ἐν ταῖς Πράξεσι, Athanasius 25 488 C ; Στεφάνου τοῦ μεγάλου μάρτυρος, 25 489 B ; ὁ μέγας Ἰώβ, Basil CCXXIII 336 B.

χρηστός: adj., *benign.*

Χρηστός occurs frequently as an epithet in the letters of Libanius. There are occasional examples in the Cappadocians and in Julian. The extent of its usage is indicated by the following examples: ὁ δὲ χρηστὸς Κυριακὸς ἥψατο πρότερον, Basil CCCXXIII 448 E and also XXI 98 B, CXXXVI 227 C, CXLI 234 D; χρηστοῦ καὶ θαυμαστοῦ πατρός, Gregory of Nyssa XI 5; τῷ μεγάλῳ καὶ χρηστῷ Ἰακώβῳ, Gregory of Nazianzus CCVII 344 B; τὸν δὲ χρηστὸν Σαλούστιον, Julian IV; Φλωρέντιος ὁ χρηστὸς καὶ τῆς ἀρετῆς φίλος, Libanius ριγ΄ 3; ὁ χρηστος Ἱλάριος, Libanius 2μζ΄ 1; also Libanius ριθ΄ 9, ψμβ΄ 1, ωπβ΄ 1, 2 1, ͵αμγ΄ 2, et passim.

UNCLASSIFIED TITLES

Titles of which the examples are too rare or too scattered to admit of any conclusions concerning their use are as follows:

ἀγαθότης: n., *Goodness.*

Ἀγαθότης is one of the less common titles of address. Only the Cappadocians and their fellow student, Julian, make use of it. Although the rarity of examples prohibits any generalization concerning its use, we may state that, of the passages in which ἀγαθότης occurs as a title, the greater number are addressed to bishops. The examples of its use for bishops are as follows: νῦν διὰ τῆς σῆς ἀγαθότητος ἔστι δυνατὸν γενέσθαι μοί τινα τῶν λυπηρῶν ἐπανόρθωσιν, Gregory of Nazianzus LXIV 128 A; ἡμεῖς δὲ παρακαλοῦμεν τὴν σὴν ἀγαθότητα, Gregory of Nazianzus CCXIX 357 B; ὑποίσομεν τῶν παρόντων ἀηδῶν τὴν δαψίλειαν ἐπ᾽ ἐλπίδι τοῦ τῆς σῆς ἀγαθότητος διὰ παντὸς μετέχειν, Gregory of Nyssa XVIII 11; ταῦτά σου τῆς ἀγαθότητος μετὰ σπουδῆς κατελήρησα τούτων ἔχων σκοπόν, ὥστε . . . , Gregory of Nyssa XXV 10.

It is applied also to a layman of official rank, Olympius, governor of Cappadocia: καὶ δι᾽ ἡμῶν προσπίπτει τῇ σῇ ἀγαθότητι, Gregory of Nazianzus CVI 205 C; καὶ ἅμα τῆς σῆς στοχαζόμενος ἀγαθότητος οὐκ ἐπαινούσης τὸ διαστάσιον, Gregory of Nazianzus CXLIV 245 C.

Gregory of Nyssa addresses it to priests: πολλὴ δὲ καὶ ἡ τῆς ὑμετέρας ἀγαθότητος εἰς ἡμᾶς ῥᾳθυμία, XVII 2.

Although ἀγαθότης is an ecclesiastical word, there are two examples of its occurrence as a title in the letters of Julian: to a priestess, τὸ πεπύσθαι με περὶ τῆς σῆς ἀγαθότητος, XXXII; to a sophist, περὶ τοῦ τὴν σὴν ἀγαθότητα πρός με ἥκειν εἴπερ διανοῇ . . . , II.

There are three cases where the station in life of the addressee is unknown. Twice St. Basil addresses it to a Theodorus who, from the context of the letter, may have been an ecclesiastic: ὃ δέ μοι πρὸς τὴν σὴν συμβέβηκεν ἀγαθότητα οὐ πόρρω τῶν εἰρημένων ἐστίν, CXXIV 214 B; ἐνόμισα εἰκόνα τῆς ἀγαθότητός σου ἐναργεστάτην ἐν τῇ τῶν εὐλαβεστάτων ἡμῶν ἀδελφῶν παρουσίᾳ ἑωρακέναι, 214 C. The third case occurs in a letter of Gregory of Nazianzus to Amphilochius. Since the letter is of uncertain date, it may have been written before his elevation to the episcopal dignity: ἅπαξ δὲ τὸν Γλαῦκον πεζεύειν μαθόντα γραμματοφόρον προσαπεστάλκαμεν τῇ ὑμετέρᾳ ἀγαθότητι, Gregory of Nazianzus XXVIII 64 A.

ἀνδρεία: n., *Fortitude*.

Isidorus uses ἀνδρεία as a title in addressing a monk: διὸ ταῦτα μὲν παρήσω, ἐκεῖνο δὲ παραινέσαιμι τῇ σῇ ἀνδρείᾳ παντόθεν ὀμματοῦν ἑαυτήν, III 228, 912 A. The title occurs in papyri.[26]

ἀνεξικακία: n., *Patience*.

The title occurs in only two instances: to the emperor, ἰδοὺ γοῦν, τῶν παροξυνόντων πεπαυμένων πέφηνεν ἡ σὴ θεοσεβὴς ἀνεξικακία, καὶ δεδείκται πᾶσιν, ὅτι μηδὲ τὴν ἀρχὴν ἐδίωκες σὺ τοὺς Χριστιανούς, Athanasius 25 641 B; to Athanasius of Alexandria, ἐπεὶ οὖν ὥρμηται νῦν γνησίως πᾶν τὸ περὶ ἡμᾶς ὑγιαῖνον κατὰ τὴν πίστιν εἰς τὴν πρὸς τοὺς ὁμοδόξους κοινωνίαν καὶ ἕνωσιν, θαρροῦντως, ἤλθομεν εἰς τὴν παράκλησίν σου τῆς ἀνεξικακίας, ἐπιστεῖλαι πᾶσιν ὑμῖν ἐπιστολὴν μίαν, Basil LXXXII 175 D.

ἀνυπέρβλητος: adj., *unsurpassable*.

Ἀνυπέρβλητος occurs in the following passage to a count: παρακέκλησο, δέσποτα ἀνυπέρβλητε, ἐπινεῦσαι πρὸς τὴν αἴτησιν, Basil CXII 205 D. The word occurs occasionally as part of a title, for example, σου τὴν ἀνυπερβλήτου τιμιότητα, Basil CCLXXV 420 D.

---

[26] Preisigke s. v.

γενναιότητος: adj., *most noble.*

We find but two occurrences of this title: ὡς δὲ συντόμως δηλῶσαι, ἧκεν ἡμῖν ὁ γενναιότατος ᾿Ανθιμος μετά τινων ἐπισκόπων, Gregory of Nazianzus L 101 B; ἔναγχος οὖν ἧκει παρὰ βασίλεως στρατηγεῖν εὐράμενος τῶν γενναιοτάτων Μαρκομάνων, Synesius CX 1492 D, to unknown persons. It occurs in papyri.[27]

ἐμμελέστατος: adj., *most gracious.*

᾿Εμμελέστατος occurs but once with reference to two gentlemen of rank, Marcianus and Marcellinus; καὶ προσφθεγγόμεθα συνεχῶς, μᾶλλον δὲ διηνεκῶς, τὴν εὐγενεστάτην καὶ ἐμμελεστάτην ὑμῶν ψυχήν, Chrysostom C 661.

ἐνδοξότης: n., *Distinction.*

There is but one illustration of the use of ἐνδοξότης as a title. It is addressed to Euryclius, patrician, ἐπιτετευγμένως ἐρρέθη περὶ τῆς σῆς ἐνδοξότητος, Nilus II 221, 361 A. The title is found in papyri.[28]

ἐπιείκεια: n., *Clemency.*

This title occurs rarely. Athanasius addresses it to the emperor: πρέσβεις πρὸς τὴν σὴν ἐπιείκειαν ἀπεστάλκαμεν, 26 697 C; διὸ δὴ ἱκετεύομεν τὴν σὴν ἐπιείκειαν, 26 700 A. Cyril of Alexandria uses it in addressing the church of Alexandria: διψῶντί μοι πάλιν τῆς ὑμῶν ἐπιεικείας τὴν πρόσρησιν, δέδοται τοῦ γράφειν καιρὸς καὶ τόπος, XXI 129 C. The title occurs once in the third person, referred to Athanasius by the emperor Constantine: ἐννοῶν τὴν ἐπιμέλειαν τῆς ἐπιεικείας αὐτοῦ, 25 361 D. ᾿Επιείκεια is found as a title in papyri.[29]

ἐπιφανέστατος: adj., *most illustrious.*

We have found but one example of the use of ἐπιφανέστατος as a title. Athanasius addresses it to the Caesars, the sons of Constantine: καὶ κατὰ τῶν δεσποτῶν ἡμῶν Κωνσταντίνου τοῦ Αὐγούστου καὶ τῶν ἐπιφανεστάτων Καισάρων παίδων αὐτοῦ, 25 385 C. The lexica note

---

[27] Preisigke s. v.
[28] Preisigke s. v.
[29] Preisigke s. v.; Moulton and Milligan s. v.

ἐπιφανέστατος as a title of the Caesars in papyri [30] and also as a title of divinities and eastern kings.[30]

εὐδοκίμησις: n., *Good Repute.*

There are the following examples of εὐδοκίμησις as a title: to monks, καὶ τῆς ὑμετέρας εὐδοκίμησις ὁ ἀγὼν πᾶσι λελάληται, Serapion 928 A; καὶ πανηγύρεως ὑπόθεσιν τὴν σὴν εὐδοκίμησιν ποιούμεθα, Isidorus V 364, 1544 D; to an unknown person, . . . εἰ μὴ ἄκρως αὐτοῦ καθάψαιτο τῆς σῆς εὐδοκιμήσεως τὸ κλέος, Isidorus V 306, 1516 A. The title is found in papyri.[31]

θειότατος: adj., *most divine.*

The title θειότατος occurs rarely. Cyril of Alexandria uses it in referring to John, bishop of Antioch, as follows: γέγραφε πρός με ὁ κύριός μου ὁ θειότατος ἐπίσκοπος τῆς 'Αντιοχέων 'Ιωάννης, LXXII 344 D. Julian applies it to the Neo-Platonic philosopher, Iamblichus, 'Ιαμβλίχου τοῦ θειοτάτου, LVIII. Libanius uses it as a title of the emperor: αἱ τοῦ θειοτάτου βασιλέως πρὸς σὲ καταλλαγαί, ϩνζ' 1; διά τοῦ θειοτάτου βασίλεως, ϩϛ' 1; cf. also ωξη' 5, ϩϛ' 1.

θειότης: n., *Divine Self.*

We have found only two passages in which the title θειότης occurs. Athanasius used it in the third person, referring to the Augusti and Caesars: προσέταξεν ἡ θειότης αὐτῶν ᾗ τάχος τοῦτο πραχθῆναι, 25 401 B. Theodoret addresses it to a person who is unidentified: οὕτω τὴν σὴν θειότητα κρῖναι τοῖς ἐμοῖς ὑπείληφα λόγοις, τοῦ φίλτρου τὴν ψῆφον ἐξενεγκόντος, II 1176 A.

θεοσεβής: adj., *godly.*

Θεοσεβής occurs twice as a title of bishops: τίνας τῶν κατὰ τὴν Μακεδονίαν θεοσεβεῖς ἐπισκόπους, Cyril of Alexandria XIII 96 C; πρὸς τὸν θεοσεβῆ ἐπίσκοπον 'Ιμέριον, Firmus V 1485 B.

καθαρότης: n., *Integrity.*

Καθαρότης is a title in the following instances: to Valerian, bishop, χάρις τῷ Κυρίῳ τῷ δόντι ἡμῖν ἀρχαίας ἀγάπης καρπὸν ἰδεῖν ἐν τῇ σῇ

---

[30] Moulton and Milligan, Preisigke, Liddell and Scott s. v.
[31] Preisigke s. v.

καθαρότητι, ὅς γε τοσοῦτον διεστὼς τῷ σώματι, συνῆψας ἡμῖν σεαυτὸν διὰ γράμματος; Basil XCI 182 D; to Olympius, prefect, μηδαμῶς, ὦ θαυμάσιε, μὴ τοῦτο παραστήτω τῇ σῇ καθαρότητι, Gregory of Nazianzus CXLVI 249 C. This title occurs in papyri.[32]

κράτιστος: adj., *most excellent*; as a substantive, *most excellent Sir*.

The examples of the title κράτιστος are infrequent. There are no instances of its use in the Epistles of the New Testament although the lexica note several illustrations elsewhere; i. e., Lk. I 3, Acts XXIII 26, XXIV 3, XXVI 25.[33] It is found also in papyri.[34] The title occurs as follows in the letters studied: to a pagan ἐπειδὴ ὁρῶ, κράτιστε Διόγνετε, ὑπερεσπουδακότα σε τὴν θεοσέβειαν τῶν Χριστιανῶν μαθεῖν, Epistle to Diognetus I; to the emperor Theodosius, δέξαι με τὸ ἀληθὲς λέγοντα, κράτιστε, Basil CCCLXV 467 A, also 467 B, 467 C, a letter which is considered unauthentic; to the emperor Constans, ἢ οὐκ οἶσθα αὐτός, ὡς Κῶνστα τοῦ κρατίστου γέγονα ἀπόγονος, Julian LXXXI,[35] a letter which is probably spurious but early. There are several examples in Libanius: πρότερον μὲν ἐθαύμαζον τὸν κράτιστον Ἑρμογένην, κα΄ 1; τῆς τοῦ κρατίστου δεῖ Σαλουτίου γνώμης, ‚αρπϛ΄ 3; cf. also ιζ΄ 1, σῃ΄ 4, νϚβ 1, ‚ασλε΄ 3, ‚αμφβ΄.

λογιώτατος: adj., *most eloquent*.

The title λογιώτατος occurs too infrequently to allow of any statement concerning its use. It appears, however, to be employed in the same manner as λογιότης, that is, for laymen who were scholars. The examples are as follows: to a layman, κατὰ τοῦ λογιωτάτου Εὐστοχίου, Basil LXXII 166 B; to rhetors, τὸν λογιώτατον τῶν κατ᾽ αὐτὴν Εὐδόξιον τὸν ῥήτορα, Gregory of Nazianzus XXXVII 77 B, and also XVII 52 A, CLXXXI 296 C; to unknown persons, Firmus XIII 1492 B; Procopius XI 2728 D, LXXXV 2784 D, XC 2788 C. There is one early example in the canonical letter of Dionysius of Alexandria to Basilides, bishop: ἀπέστειλάς μοι, πιστότατε καὶ λογιώτατε υἱέ μου, 1272 B.

---

[32] Preisigke s. v.
[33] Sophocles, Moulton and Milligan, Thayer s. v.
[34] Preisigke s. v.
[35] Letter LXXXI is found also in the Basilian corpus as letter XL.

μεγαλειότης: n., *Majesty.*

As a title μεγαλειότης occurs but once, to a layman of high rank: σκώπτεις τὴν Ἀλυπιανὴν ἡμῖν, ὡς μικράν, καὶ τῆς σῆς μεγαλειότητος ἀναξίαν, ὦ μάκρε σύ, καὶ ἀμέτρητε, καὶ πελώριε, τό τε εἶδος καὶ τὴν ἀλκήν, Gregory of Nazianzus XII 44 C.

μεγαλοψυχία: n., *Magnanimity.*

The passages in which μεγαλοψυχία is found as a title are as follows: to a bishop, πρέπει οὖν ἂν τῇ σῇ μεγαλοψυχίᾳ τὸ μὲν φιλόνεικον ἑτέροις παραχωρεῖν, Basil LIX 154 B; to a general, οὐκ ἂν ἐπέστελλον, ἀλλ' αὐτὸς παρὰ τὴν σὴν μεγαλοψυχίαν ἐβάδιζον δυοῖν ἕνεκεν, Basil CXII 204 A; to a priestess, ἐν δευτέρῳ τῇ σῇ μεγαλοψυχίᾳ χάριν ἔσχον, Julian XXXIV. There are three doubtful cases: Gregory of Nazianzus LXXIX 149 B, Theodoret XXIX 1208 B, and XXXVI 1213 C.

ὁμοψυχία: n., *Unanimity.*

This title is found twice in Athanasius: καὶ τοῦτο γὰρ γινωσκέτω ὑμῶν ἡ ὁμοψυχία, ὅτι κρίσει . . . , 25 316 C; καὶ τοῦτο γὰρ γινωσκέτω ὑμῶν ἡ ὁμοψυχία, . . . 25 321 D.

ὁμόψυχος: adj., *consensient.*

Ὁμόψυχος occurs in the following passages: τῷ τιμιωτάτῳ ἀδελφῷ καὶ ὁμοψύχῳ Ἀλεξάνδρῳ, Ἀλέξανδρος ἐν Κυρίῳ χαίρειν, Alexander of Alexandria 548 A; κυρίῳ ἀγαπητῷ υἱῷ καὶ ὁμοψύχῳ συλλειτουργῷ Ἀθανασίῳ Ἀλέξανδρος ἐπίσκοπος ἐν Κυρίῳ χαίρειν, Athanasius 25 368 A; τοῖς θεοφιλεστάτοις καὶ ὁσιωτάτοις ἀδελφοῖς συλλειτουργοῖς κατὰ τὴν Ἰταλίαν καὶ Γαλλίαν ὁμοψύχοις ἐπισκόποις, Basil XCII 183 C. Its use as a title is doubtful.

περιπόθητος: adj., *much desired.*

Two instances of the use of this title occur in Basil: πολὺν χρόνον ἀπεσιωπήσαμεν πρὸς ἀλλήλους, ἀδελφοὶ τιμώτατοι ἡμῖν καὶ περιπόθητοι, CCIV 302 E; ἀλλ' ὑμεῖς, ὦ ἀγαπητοὶ ἡμῖν καὶ περιπόθητοι, γένεσθε τῶν μὲν τραυματιῶν ἰατροί, CCXLII 372 C. Compare with this, the use of ἐπιπόθητος in Philip. IV 1; ἀδελφοί μου ἀγαπητοὶ καὶ ἐπιπόθητοι.

πιστότατος: adj., *most faithful*.

Πιστότατος is used as a title in the following passages: to the wife of the deacon Ambrose, ἀσπάζεται δέ σε καὶ ἡ πιστοτάτη σύμβιος αὐτοῦ Μαρκέλλα, Origen 85 D; to the bishop Basilides, ἀπέστειλάς μοι, πιστότατε καὶ λογιώτατε υἷε μου, Dionysius of Alexandria 1272 B; to an unknown Spirantius, Σπειράντιον τὸν πιστότατον, Athanasius 25 604 C; to the laity of Constantinople, τῷ εὐλαβεστάτῳ καὶ πιστοτάτῳ καὶ φιλοχρίστῳ λαῷ τῆς ἐν Κωνσταντινουπόλει ἁγίας τοῦ Θεοῦ Ἐκκλησίας ἡ σύνοδος, Theodoret CLVI 1448 C.

The positive πιστός is quoted by Milligan as a title in a number of Syrian inscriptions and this form appears in the Epistles of the New Testament: διὰ τοῦτο ἔπεμψα ὑμῖν Τιμόθεον, ὅς ἐστίν μου τέκνον ἀγαπητὸν καὶ πιστὸν ἐν Κυρίῳ, I Cor. IV 17; τὰ κατ' ἐμὲ πάντα γνωρίσει ὑμῖν Τύχικος ὁ ἀγαπητὸς ἀδελφὸς καὶ πιστὸς διάκονος καὶ σύνδουλος ἐν Κυρίῳ, Col. IV 7; σὺν Ὀνησίμῳ τῷ πιστῷ καὶ ἀγαπητῷ ἀδελφῷ, Col. IV 9.

πολυπόθητος: adj., *greatly desired*.

The word appears once in address: γίνωσκε μέντοι ὡς ἀληθῶς εὐλαβέστατε καὶ πολυπόθητε ἡμῖν ἀδελφέ, Basil CLVI 246 B.

πρᾳότατε: substantive, *most clement friend*.

The title occurs as follows: οὐ τὰ κατὰ διάνοιαν οἶδεν, ὦ πρᾳότατε, ὁ διάβολος, Isidorus III 156, 852 A; ὦ πρᾳότατε, Libanus υμ' 3.

προσφιλέστατος: adj., *most dearly beloved*; as a substantive; *most dearly beloved friend*.

Προσφιλέστατος is found as a title in the following passages: πάτερ προσφιλέστατε, addressed to Athanasius, 25 624 C; to a deacon, ὦ προσφιλέστατε, Isidorus V 112, 1389 D; to a lector, οὐ τὸ καλεῖσθαι ἁπλῶς πρωτότοκον, ὦ προσφιλέστατε, Isidorus II 47, 489 A; to the laity of Alexandria, πρὸς τὴν προσφιλεστάτην ὑμῶν θεοσέβειαν, quoted in Athanasius 25 405 C; to a layman, ἀλλ' ἔρρωσό μοι ἐν Κυρίῳ, υἱῶν προσφιλέστατε, Nilus III 43, 413 C; ἔρρωσό μοι, ἀδελφὲ ποθεινότατε καὶ προσφιλέστατε, Julian LII, also LIII; cf. also Synesius CXXXIX 1532 C.

Moulton and Milligan state that προσφιλέστατος is common in epitaphs.

σεβασμώτατος: adj., *most august.*

The title is found only in the letters of Synesius. The passages are as follows: to Theophilus, bishop of Alexandria, πάτερ σεβασμώτατε, LXVII 1417 B, and 1429 A; to Hypatia, the philosopher, ἄσπασαι τὴν σεβασμωτάτην καὶ θεοφιλεστάτην φιλόσοφον, IV 1341 B; to an unknown Marcianus, πρόσειπε παρ' ἐμοῦ πάνυ πολλὰ τὸν σεβασμώτατον Μαρκιανόν, C 1472 B. It is also found in papyri.[36]

σοφία: n., *Wisdom.*

As a title, σοφία occurs rarely in the literature examined. The examples we have noted are as follows: to a bishop, ἀρκεῖ ἐπὶ τῆς εἰκόνος ἐᾶσαι τὸν λόγον, οὔτε τῆς σῆς σοφίας ἐπιτρεπούσης τι πλέον, Basil LXXXII 175 C; to a layman of high rank, σκοπησάτω τοίνυν ἡ ὑμετέρα σοφία τὴν τῆς ἀδικίας ὑπερβολήν, Theodoret XLII 1220 A; to persons who are not known, ἐπειδὴ δὲ μεμήνυκας, ἃ μήτε ἐγὼ σεσίγηκα καὶ τῆς σῆς σοφίας τῷ δοκεῖν τἀληθῆ μέμψασθαι περιγίνεται, Isidorus IV 205, 1293 C; ἡ τῆς ὑμετέρας σοφίας ἐπιστολή, Procopius XLII 2752 A; Παλλαδίῳ τῷ χρηστῷ κέρδος μὲν ὁ τρόπος, μέγα δὲ καὶ τὸ παρὰ τῆς σῆς σοφίας κεῖσθαι τοιαύτην ἐπιστολὴν τῆς ἀληθείας ὅτι μάλιστα ἔχομεν, Libanius ⳥ 1. It is found as a title in papyri.[37]

σπουδή: n., *Zeal.*

The emperor is addressed with this title in Athanasius 25 629 D: ἀναγκαῖον δὲ ὅμως εἰπεῖν, ἵνα ἡ σὴ φιλόχριστος σπουδὴ καὶ θεοσέβεια μάθῃ.

στερρότης: n., *Constancy.*

The title occurs as follows: γράμματα πρὸς τὴν σὴν στερρότητα διεπεμψάμεθα, addressed to Athanasius, 25 341 B; also, ταῦτα τὰ γράμματα πρὸς τὴν σὴν στερρότητα δεδώκαμεν, 25 341 C; ὡς ἀντιγράφων τῇ σῇ στερρότητι, 25 369 A, and 26 792 B. It is also given to laymen of high rank: καὶ ὀφειλόμενον τοῖς τὴν στερρότητά σου εἰς τὴν ὑπὲρ ὧν πεπόνθαι βοήθειαν ἐπικαλούμενος, Basil LXXXVI 178 E; ταῦτα εἰ μὲν ἀνεκτά, ἐγεγκάτω μὲν ἡ σὴ στερρότης, Gregory of Nazianzus CXXV 220 B.

---

[36] Preisigke s. v.
[37] Moulton and Milligan s. v.; Preisigke s. v.

συνετώτατος : adj., *most intelligent.*

Συνετώτατος is used as a title in three instances: to the bishop Basilides, σὺ συνετώτατέ μου υἱέ, Dionysius of Alexandria, 1288 C; to monks, τοῖς εὐσεβεστάτοις καὶ συνετωτάτοις συντετυχότες μονάζουσιν, Theodoret CXLI 1365 C; to a citizen of senatorial rank who had displeased the emperor, ὦ συνετώτατε Διονύσιε, Julian L.

τίμιος : adj., *honorable.*

We find two instances in which the adjective τίμιος is used as a title: to the clergy of Iconium, πάντα τὸν τίμιον κλῆρον καὶ τοὺς συνόντας τῇ θεοσεβείᾳ σου ἀσπαζόμεθα διὰ σοῦ, Basil CCXVIII 331 E; to Libanius, apparently a layman, τοῦ τιμίου μοι καὶ ἐνδοξοτάτου ἀδελφοῦ Λιβανίου ἐνταῦθα ἀφιγμένου, Chrysostom CCXXV 735.

φιλία : n., *Affection.*

Gregory of Nazianzus has the following examples of the use of φιλία as a title: to Gregory, archon, σφόδρα ἡμῖν ἀναγκαίαν, καὶ πρὸς τῆς σῆς φιλίας αἰτῶ τὰ τῶν φίλων, CXCV 320 A; χαίρω δὲ ὅτι μοι καὶ τὴν σὴν προξενεῖ φιλίαν, CCXXVIII 372 B.

φιλομαθέστατε : adj., *most wisdom-loving*; as a substantive, *most wisdom-loving Sir.*

This title occurs as follows: to the emperor, φιλομαθέστατε βασιλεῦ, Athanasius 25 620 A; to a lector, ὦ φιλομαθέστατε, Isidorus II 3, 457 B.

φίλος : adj., *dear*; as a substantive, *my friend.*

Φίλος is found rarely as a term of address among Christian writers, except in the letters of Isidorus. The pagan Libanius, however, uses it frequently. The term is addressed to ecclesiastics as follows: to a bishop, ὦ φίλος, Isidorus V 92, 1380 A; to a deacon, ὦ φίλε, Isidorus III 312, 977 C; to a monk, μὴ ἀγνόει, ὦ φίλος, Isidorus III 227, 909 B.

It is applied to the laity as follows: ἐπειδήπερ ἠρώτησας, ὦ φίλε, διὰ τοῦ γράμματος . . . , Gregory of Nyssa II 1; χρῆ, ὦ φίλε, καὶ πρὸς πολεμίους ἱκέοντας σπένδεσθαι, Isidorus II 55, 497 D; τῆς φίλης Ὑπατίας μεμνήσομαι, Synesius CXXIV 1504 C. Cf. also Isidorus III

133, 832 C; 195, 881 A; IV 208, 1301 C; V 544, 1632 C; Julian XII, LX.

For further references, cf. Athanasius 27 12 A; Isidorus III 279, 956 C; IV 92, 1153 B; 205, 1293 B; V 551, 1633 D; Libanius σκϛ′ 1, σιη′ 8, το′ 1, ψμη′ 1, ϡλη′ 3, ,αλα′ 1, et passim.

φιλοσοφώτατος: adj., *wisdom-loving, contemplative.*

There are only two instances of the use of φιλοσοφώτατος as a title, both addressed to laymen of distinction: μετὰ τὸν ἡμερώτατον καὶ φιλοσοφώτατον Πεντάδιον, Synesius CXXVII 1508 A; ἐπὶ τοῦ θεοφιλεστάτου καὶ φιλοσοφωτάτου καὶ μακαριωτάτου Ἰουλιανοῦ, Athanasius 26 820 C

χρηστότατος: adj., *most benign.*

The adjective χρηστότατος is used in the following passage, probably as a title of address: κύριε πάντων χάριν χρηστότατε, to Athanasius in 25 368 B.

SUMMARY

I

The Epistles of the New Testament present the earliest evidence concerning the Christian use of titles. I have found that these Epistles contain very few titles and that they are always simple adjectives, Christian in tone, such as ἀγαπητός, ἅγιος, γνήσιος, ἐπιποθητός, πιστός, or nouns expressing close relationship such as ἀδελφός, τέκνον, and υἱός. As for ἄνθρωπε and κυρία, which also occur, the former was used to express indignation, and the latter had probably at this time acquired the polite signification of *madam* or *lady*. There are no examples of highly complimentary superlatives, nor of personified qualities used as titles.

In the Epistles of the Apostolic Fathers, i. e. Pseudo-Barnabas, Clement of Rome, Ignatius, Polycarp, and Irenaeus, the use of titles is much the same. There is the addition of μακάριος and γλυκύτατος. Ἀγάπη occurs with a use approaching that of a title in the Epistle of Barnabas and in the letters of St. Ignatius.

For the authors who fall within the third century, i. e. Origen, Alexander of Jerusalem, Sextus Julianus Africanus, Dionysius of Alexandria, and the author of the Epistle to Diognetus, the evidence of the letters is scanty, but uniform and significant. Besides the older forms ἀγαπητός, ἅγιος, μακάριος, υἱός, I have found the following titles which show the introduction of the superlative adjectives, ἄριστος, αἰδεσιμώτατος, λογιώτατος, πιστότατος, σπουδαιότατος, συνετώτατος, one noun title of humility μετριότης, the positive adjective καλός, and the nouns κύριος and πάπας.

With the authors who wrote within the fourth century, namely Alexander of Alexandria and Eusebius of Caesarea, I have found a decided change in the use of titles. The noun title and the familiar superlative adjective title now become comparatively frequent—εὐλάβεια, εὐλαβέστατος, εὐσεβέστατος, θεοσέβεια, θεοσεβέστατος, σοφώτατος. Ἀγαπητός is still used.

Beginning with the Golden Age of Patristic Literature, there are extensive collections of letters and a correspondingly frequent

105

use of conventional titles. The more voluminous authors who make use of the familiar titles—personified qualities and superlative adjectives—are Athanasius, Basil, Gregory of Nazianzus, Gregory of Nyssa, John Chrysostom, Cyril of Alexandria, Firmus of Caesarea, John of Antioch, and Theodoret. Amphilochius, Cyril of Jerusalem, Peter of Alexandria, Nestorius, Proclus of Constantinople wrote far fewer letters, but in their small compass, these same familiar titles are found. In general, the earlier authors of the Golden Age, Athanasius and the Cappadocians, are less profuse in their use of titles than the later ones, from John Chrysostom to Theodoret. In a period in which many of the titles were not strictly conventionalized, an author was at liberty to use his individual term in addressing a given personage. St. Basil, for instance, uses σεμνότης in addressing bishops, while Theodoret uses φιλοθεΐα. Serapion of Thmuis and Theophilus of Alexandria are more sparing in their use of quality titles, but they use noun titles of relationship, adjectives, and substantives, a representative number of times. Arius uses only the following titles: ἄνθρωπος Θεοῦ, κύριος, μακάριος, πάπας, ποθεινότατος. Isidorus, Nilus, and Synesius comprise a group in this period who differ from the rest in their use of titles. With them, the quality title of address and the superlative adjective are rare; and the sophistic substantive title, such as βέλτιστε, ὦ φιλότης, ὦ μακάριε, ᾧ θαυμάσιε, λῷστε, γενναῖε, ἄνθρωπε, occurs commonly. The sophist Procopius uses titles sparingly. His titles are: θεοσέβεια, μέγεθος, σοφία, σοφώτατος, λογιώτατος, θεοσεβέστατος, and the sophistic terms of address which he uses by preference, βέλτιστε, θαυμάσιε, λῷστε.

From the period of decline, the letters of two authors remain to us. The synodal letter of Gennadius is quite representative and contains examples of the common titles μακάριος, ὁσιότης, θεοφιλέστατος. The writings current under the name of Dionysius the Areopagite contain only the following three titles: ἄνθρωπε, γενναῖε, καλός.

As for the pagans whose works were studied, we find that Julian's use of titles, though rare, agrees fairly well with that of the Christian writers, but he does not use any of the more strikingly ecclesiastical titles. His titles are these: ἀγαθότης, αἰδεσιμώτατος, αὔγουστος, βασίλεια, διάθεσις, ἡμερότης, μακαρίτης, προσφιλέστατος, μεγαλοψυχία, φρόνησις, ποθεινότατος, φιλανθρωπία; the sophistic type, βέλτιστος, γενναῖος, θαυμάσιος, κεφαλή, καλός; and his peculiar usage ἀγαθώτατος and φιλικώτατος. Libanius uses the common sophistic terms of address such as: ἀγαθός, ἄριστος, βέλτιστος, θαυμάσιος, θαυμαστός, γενναῖος, καλός, κεφαλή, μακάριος χρηστός, σοφός, φίλος, φίλτατος; also καλὸς κἀγαθός, κράτιστος, μέγας, πρᾶότατος, φιλανθρωπότατος and one peculiar to himself, δαιμόνιε. Two noun titles occur, ἡμερότης and πρᾳότης.

II

Of the titles found in the letters of the first five centuries, the following are recorded by Liddell and Scott as terms of address in classical literature: ἀγαθέ, ἄνθρωπε, βέλτιστε, γενναῖε, γλυκύτατε, δαιμόνιε, δέσποτα, θαυμάσιε, θαυμαστέ, καλός, καλὸς κἀγαθός, λῷστε, μακάριε, μέγας, πάπας (children to their father), πάτερ, τέκνον, ὦ φιλότης, ψυχή. Except δεσπότης, μέγας, πάπας, πατήρ, τέκνον and ψυχή, I have found these titles for the most part in authors of sophistic tendency such as Libanius, Nilus, Isidorus, Synesius, Procopius, and Pseudo-Dionysius. Θαυμάσιε, ἄνθρωπε, and κεφαλή occur also in typically ecclesiastical authors, apparently as a device to obtain a literary finish. The literary nature of these terms of address is confirmed by the fact that they are not found in any of the non-literary sources.

III

The following is a survey of the conventions observed by Byzantine writers in their use of titles.

Emperor

Titles addressed exclusively to the emperor: αὔγουστος, βασίλεια, βασίλειον, γαληνότατος, γαληνότης, εὐσεβής, καλλίνικος, κορυφή, κράτος, μέγιστος, νικητής, σεβαστός.
Titles addressed to the emperor with rare exceptions: εὐσέβεια, εὐσεβέστατος, φιλανθρωπία, φιλόχριστος.
Titles addressed to the emperor as well as to persons of other

stations in life: θεοσέβεια, θεοσεβέστατος, θεοφιλέστατος, θεοφιλής, δεσπότης, ἡμερότης.

Titles of the emperor addressed to the empress: αὐγούστη, βασίλεια, εὐσέβεια, εὐσεβεστάτη, θεοφιλεστάτη, γαληνότης, φιλόχριστος.

Bishops

Titles addressed exclusively to bishops: ἐπίσημος (rare); πάπας.

Titles addressed to bishops with rare exceptions: ἁγιότης, ἁγιώτατος, ἁγιωσύνη, ἄνθρωπος τοῦ Θεοῦ, ὁσιώτατος, πατήρ.

Titles used generally for bishops: θεοσέβεια, θεοσεβέστατος, ὁσιότης, φιλοθεΐα.

Titles addressed to bishops and the emperor: θεοφιλέστατος, θεοφιλής, δεσπότης.

Titles addressed to bishops and other clergy: ἀγάπη, ἀγαπητός, εὐλάβεια, εὐλαβέστατος.

Titles addressed to bishops and the laity: αἰδεσιμώτατος, δεσπότης, ὀρθότης, σύνεσις, τελειότης, φρόνησις, χρηστότης, σεμνοπρέπεια, σεμνότης, σεμνότατος.

Deacons

Titles addressed exclusively to deacons, but found rarely: γλυκύτης, σπουδαιότατος.

Laymen

Titles addressed to laymen of official rank:

(1) Exclusively: δική, ἐξουσία, ἡμερώτατος, λαμπρότατος, λαμπρότης, μέγεθος, περίβλεπτος.

(2) With rare exceptions: καλοκἀγαθία, μεγαλόνοια.

Titles addressed to laymen of high rank:

(1) Exclusively: ἐνδοξότατος, μεγαλοπρέπεια, μεγαλοπρεπέστατος.

(2) With rare exceptions: ἄριστε, θαυμασιότης, θαυμασιώτατος, μεγαλοφυΐα.

Titles addressed to men of letters:

(1) Exclusively: λογιότης, παίδευσις.

(2) Not exclusively: ἐλλογιμώτατος.

Titles addressed to laymen and the emperor: δεσπότης, ἡμερότης, φιλανθρωπία.

Titles addressed to laymen and bishops: αἰδεσιμώτατος, δεσπότης, ὀρθότης, σύνεσις, τελειότης, φρόνησις, χρηστότης, σεμνοπρέπεια, σεμνότατος, σεμνότης.

Titles addressed to laymen and laywomen: εὐγένεια, εὐγενέστατος, κοσμιότης.

Women

Titles addressed exclusively to women: δέσποινα, κοσμιώτατος, κυρία.

Titles addressed not exclusively to women: διάθεσις, ἐμμέλεια, εὐγένεια, εὐγενέστατος, θαυμασιότης (in Theodoret), σεμνοπρέπεια, σεμνότης, σεμνότατος, τιμιότης (in Chrysostom), τιμώτατος (in Chrysostom).

Other Conventions

Titles of humility equivalent to the first person: βραχύτης, εὐτέλεια, εὐτελέστατος, μετριότης, οὐδένεια, σμικρότης, ταπείνωσις.

Titles used in referring to deceased persons: μακάριος, μακαρίτης, μακαριώτατος.

Titles used without distinction of class: διάθεσις, ἐμμέλεια, κεφαλή, κύριος, ποθεινότατος, σοφός, σοφώτατος, τιμιότης, τιμώτατος.

The foregoing summary yields the following broad generalizations:

I. The custom of using noun titles of quality and superlative adjectives and substantives as titles seems to be of Byzantine origin,[1] and to have arisen in the early fourth century.

II. Classical terms of address were continued in later letters only as a literary device.

III. The conventions governing the application of certain titles to certain classes of society were fairly rigid.

[1] The term *Byzantine*, in this study refers only to the fourth, fifth, and part of the sixth, centuries.

INDEX OF CLASSES ADDRESSED

INDEX VERBORUM

111